How to Invest in USA Real Estate

A Complete Guide To Buy, Rehab, And Manage Out-Of-State Rental Properties To Create Wealth And Passive Income, Even If You Live On The Other Side Of The World

MICHELE BRIZI

Text Copyright © [Michele Brizi]

Legal & Disclaimer

The information contained in this book and its contents is not designed to replace or take the place of any form of medical or professional advice; and is not meant to replace the need for independent medical, financial, legal or other professional advice or services, as may be required. The content and information in this book has been provided for educational and entertainment purposes only.

The content and information contained in this book has been compiled from sources deemed reliable, and it is accurate to the best of the Author's knowledge, information and belief. However, the Author cannot guarantee its accuracy and validity and cannot be held liable for any errors and/or omissions. Further, changes are periodically made to this book as and when needed. Where appropriate and/or necessary, you must consult a professional (including but not limited to your doctor, attorney, financial advisor or such other professional advisor) before using any of the suggested remedies, techniques, or information in this book.

Upon using the contents and information contained in this book, you agree to hold harmless the Author from and against any damages, costs, and expenses, including any legal fees potentially resulting from the application of any of the information provided by this book. This disclaimer applies to any loss, damages or injury caused by the use and application, whether directly or indirectly, of any advice or information presented, whether for breach of contract, tort, negligence, personal injury, criminal intent, or under any other cause of action.

You agree to accept all risks of using the information presented inside this book. You agree that by continuing to read this book, where appropriate and/or necessary, you shall consult a professional (including but not limited to your doctor, attorney, or financial advisor or such other advisor as needed) before using any of the suggested remedies, techniques, or information in this book.

Table of Contents

How to Invest in USA Real Estate

MICHELE BRIZI

No one can do anything precious in life without a loving and supportive family.

I would be lost without Romina, Alessandro and Luca.

Chapter 1. Introduction

The following chapters will discuss all the steps that you need to take in order to become successful with real estate investing.

There are many options that you can decide to go with when it comes to investing your money. But **none offer all the options, and are as rewarding, as working with real estate.** From flipping homes to using rental properties for a long-term profit, you will be able to find the method that is right for you.

This guidebook is going to spend some time exploring the world of real estate investing, and all of the cool things that you can do with it. We will look at some of the benefits of investing in real estate, the differences between rental property investing and house flipping, how to understand the market cycle and how it can help you to pick the right times to purchase and sell the properties, and even the importance of networking.

From there, we will explore the steps that you need to take to finance this investment, how to do your own calculations to make sure that the property is a smart move, how to complete the inspections to ensure that you are able to get a property without a ton of work that needs to be done, and how to close on the deal!

To end this guidebook, there will be a discussion on how to handle your rental property, including how you will find the best tenants to move in, the importance of signing a lease, how to manage these properties and the contracts that you have to use.

Or, if you choose to invest in flipping homes, we will talk about the steps that you can take to get in and out and sell the property quickly.

And finally, if you really want to see this investment grow, then it is important to take some of the profits and reinvest them in yourself.

This guidebook will take some time to discuss this important step in growing your new business.

When you are ready to start putting your money to work for you, and ensuring that you are able to make some good profits in no time in real estate, whether you want to flip homes or do rental properties, make sure to check out this guidebook to get started!

Chapter 2. Who Should You Buy Properties From?

Knowing who to buy from in real estate is another very essential aspect of a real estate investment.

This is because where you purchase the property you want to invest in has a lot to do with how successful your investment is going to be.

If you purchase from the wrong source, it could lead in losses and if you purchase from the right source, it could mean high returns for you.

For this reason, this will be discussing some key strategies to utilize in real estate investment.

Typically, there are five types of scenarios one should focus on before and during the investment process.

These are:

- Purchasing foreclosures owned by a bank

- Purchasing from owners that have no equity

- Buying from owners that have equity

- Purchasing foreclosed homes at auction

- Purchasing from owners that have equity but are absentees

Purchasing Foreclosures Owned by Banks

Bank-owned foreclosures, also known as REO, are properties that have gone through the foreclosure process, and no one showed interest during its auctioning.

Then, the bank tries to sell off the property through real estate.

The bank does this by getting a licensed real estate agent to help them to list the property to enable quick sales.

The agent then lists the property on a multiple listing service (MLS), and people begin to show interest in the property by sending in their offers just like they do at other properties.

The of offers and supervision of the sales process is done by an asset manager who has the right to accept or reject offers during the sales process.

Any offer accepted by the asset manager is usually signed and finally approved by leading bank officials.

Once the offer has been approved, the contract will be signed, and the property will be closed.

It takes a minimum of three to six weeks for the closing process to be completed.

Purchasing from Owners with No Equity

Owners with no equity are owners that couldn't meet up with the payment of their mortgage and as such, has a loan debt that is more than the cost of the property.

These homeowners are left with no option but to begin a short sale process.

The short sale process is a process that starts with the homeowner authorizing the bank or any other lender to dispose of their home at a lesser value than the amount being owed the lender.

The short sale process is beneficial to banks because it's cheap and requires little time.

This is why they mostly pick short sale over a foreclosure as foreclosure requires them to invest their time and money.

Also, at the end of the short sale, both the owner of the home and the bank wins but foreclosure may result in lower sales of the property, more economical than they would get from a short sale.

Purchasing from Owners That Have Equity

Some personal issues or situations may be too difficult to handle by the owner of a property.

These issues range from health problems, financial problems, divorce, death, or a change of environment.

This mostly results in selling off the property at a price lower than the actual cost of the property.

Buying from people experiencing financial issues may be difficult because they could owe a lot more than the value of their property as a mortgage.

With this, selling at a fair price becomes unrealistic and offsetting their mortgage becomes a problem. But for others that owe just a fraction of the value of their property as a mortgage, you can get a very reasonable price.

These homeowners are with little debt, and as such, their property has equity.

This is why they usually want to sell as soon as possible to get money to attend to their needs and pay off their mortgage at the same time.

Buying from these kinds of people helps you a great deal as you'll have the opportunity to negotiate well and make as much profit as you want in the long run.

Therefore, it's a solution where everyone benefits.

Purchasing Foreclosed Homes at Auction

Buying from foreclosure during auctioning is excellent for an investor that has years of experience.

New investors are not advised to use this option as issues may arise.

Experienced investors will be able to tell if a property is worth buying and will most likely have access to many great deals.

An inexperienced investor, on the other hand, may not be able to understand what it takes and as a result, may end up in severe financial losses at the end.

This method of buying a property can be beneficial in the long run, but it also comes with risk.

As soon as a foreclosed property become yours after the auctioning, the property's debts, claims, and liens are automatically transferred to you as the owner.

Purchasing from Owners with Equity but Are Absentees

Absentee owners are homeowners or landlords that rented out their building as a form of generating income while living in another state, country, or locality.

Some of these landlords do these when the home they inherit has issues, and they couldn't sell it off or buy a property to generate income.

The only way to achieve this is through rent, and that's precisely what an absentee landlord does.

How to Know the Best Option That Suits You?

Knowing the best option that suits you and the factors to determine to know the best option to pick is very important.

As a result, consider the following before settling down for any of the options.

Your Desired Time Frame

Ask yourself questions on how long you want the project completed.

Is it a project you want to complete as soon as possible or a project that you want to be completed in a few months?

If you're not particular about time duration, REO or short sale is the best choice for you. If you're interested in a quicker project, get an auctioned property. In all, the timeframe also helps you to decide on the type of seller you need to choose.

Your Nature

What kind of person are you?

Do you love interacting with people?

Do you put yourself in other people's shoes to know how they feel?

If your answers to these questions are yes, then this could mean that you are the type of person that can work with homeowners.

If no is your answer, you should try other options that don't involve homeowners.

It is essential to check your personality and its effect on a business before selecting your seller.

Your Location

Another factor to consider is where you reside.

Do you live in a place with many homeowners that have equity?

If you do, watch out for homeowners that are reluctant to pay or are in trouble.

Alternatively, if you have many REO deals on your MLS, it is an excellent opportunity for you.

When looking out for sellers, your place of residence and the state of the real estate market in such area will determine the type of sellers you get.

As soon as you're done knowing the best seller for you and whom to buy from, the next step is to find out how to locate great real estate investment deals, and this will be in the coming chapter.

Chapter 3. Rehab Houses

Rehabbing homes is one of the priciest projects real estate investors can execute.

It is challenging and daunting for real estate investors at all levels, but more challenging for investors that are just starting.

This is because it involves buying a property, getting it renovated, and putting it up for sale for the value it is actually worth.

Rehabbing is a job that does not get mastered so quickly.

Also, it needs an exceptional level of attention to details.

It, however, is one of the most profitable investment alternatives in real estate.

That being said, one question that is always asked by newbies about real estate investment is the process involved in rehabbing a house while on a budget.

Experience, as well as working capital, are needed to successfully rehab a house. Rehabbing is not a phenomenon you should step right into without making adequate plans.

To get the best out of rehabbing, it is vital that investors pay a lot of attention to due diligence before setting out. This includes going through all the alternatives they have.

Although rehabbing can be very financially rewarding, it is quite complicated and should not be treated carefully.

Having learned this, let's take a more detailed look into what a home rehab is all about.

What Exactly Is a House Rehab?

Basically, house rehab is a process in which a property is improved upon to make it have a better market value.

Doing this alters the condition of the property from bad to satisfactory and sometimes perfect. This is usually done without any major change to the basic plan.

Before moving on with a real estate rehab, investors have to comprehend all that is involved in rehabbing.

The first thing every investor has to know is rehabbing is in three categories. There are fix and flip, rental rehab, and personal rehab. Investors have to understand this as these different approaches will have a significant effect on profit, and the amount that is put into financing the project.

What Is the Cost of Rehabbing a House?

When rehabbing a house, you should be ready to spend between $20,000 and $75,000 and above.

This amount will be spent on labor, materials, and permit costs.

Get started by knowing how much capital you have at your disposal as this will help you locate a rehab project that is not above your budget.

This way, you can choose the type of property you are interested in investing in based on what your budget is.

The next thing to do is to start taking a tour of prospective properties.

While you do this, ensure that you are on the lookout for properties that need to be renovated and the type of project that will be involved in this. This way, investors can come up with the exact amount needed to rehab the house.

How Much Time Is Needed to Rehab a Home?

Rehabbing a property can be done in as little as six weeks. It might also last as long as six months. There is no specific time frame.

There are many factors regarding the time that will be needed to completely rehab a house is dependent on.

Some of these factors are:

- The vendors you are working with

- The exact renovation project

- The property size

It is vital that you consider the factors above prior to buying a given property as this is one way to perfectly understand a particular rehab project.

Researching how rapidly properties get bought in your market will not be a bad idea. This will give you an idea of how long you have to wait for the property to get sold when you are done with rehabbing.

Investing in undeveloped land is within the reach of beginning investors, but you'll need expert counsel to guide you through the many laws and regulations associated with land development.

Large land tracts can be good investments if you are very familiar with the area and have a good feel for what the land might be useful for now or in the future.

You can hold the investment until the per-acre market value reaches a point where it makes sense to sell, or you can move forward with some type of development

Lots for Manufactured Housing

One development option is to build lots for manufactured housing, which may be rented to people who own manufactured homes.

Check local ordinances carefully before you embark on a development for manufactured housing. If you can find the right land, with utilities that are readily available, this type of development can be a lucrative investment.

Recreational Vehicle Parks

An RV campground can be a basic facility that caters to travelers who need a place to stop for a single night, or it can be a full-service park with a swimming pool, miniature golf, and any other amenity you'd like to add. Most RV parks offer concrete pads and utility connections.

They can be located along a major highway or in a tourist destination. Research existing RV campgrounds to learn about the typical amenities and costs that travelers encounter in different areas. The resources in Appendix C will help you locate RV networks.

Self-Storage Centers

We all have too much stuff. That's probably one reason that self-storage centers are so popular.

Metal buildings built on concrete slabs are the most common configuration for these popular units, and unless you wish to offer climate-controlled areas, the buildings you rent don't even have to be heated or electrified.

Developing a piece of raw land in a commercial area can be complex or simple, depending on the project you plan to undertake.

In some areas, development is controlled on a local level; in others, the state is more involved.

Your specific project could also be subject to federal regulations. No matter what you plan to do with the land, be sure your plans conform to all applicable laws and ordinances.

Before you make final plans for the property, you must research zoning and environmental issues in order to find out if there are limitations on land use.

Even if zoning isn't an issue, deed restrictions might prevent you from using the land for specific purposes.

A deed could state that the property cannot be used for industrial purposes. A deed might even prevent a specific kind of business from being built on the land.

For instance, the former owner might also own a nearby lawn-and-garden center. Before selling the land, he inserts a clause stating that the land cannot be used to operate a lawn-and-garden company.

It's always important to analyze a property's deed to help determine how the land can be used.

Questions about environmental issues, such as the presence of protected wetlands, are another important issue that should be resolved before you buy a tract of land.

Collecting rents from tenants can be a headache, and some tenants who stop paying may never retrieve their goods.

It isn't unusual for storage centers to auction goods left by tenants in order to cover past-due storage bills.

Protect yourself with tenant deposits and a good rental agreement, and choose a great location to see excellent returns from a storage center investment.

Finding Expert Advice

This chapter has touched on only the basic details about investing in commercial properties.

As you become more involved in real estate, you'll encounter many types of properties and an endless number of ideas for potential investments.

No matter which ones you choose to pursue, do your homework and always get expert advice before moving forward with an offer.

Here are a few of the people you might contact for advice about commercial properties:

- Commercial real-estate agents can help you find comparable properties in order to determine value and can keep you informed of new listings on the market.

- Staff at your local planning board and other similar agencies are important contacts for information about land development, zoning, and many other issues.

- Staff at your county courthouse can show you how to view tax maps of land and find public information regarding the current owner's mailing address.

- Surveyors and appraisers provide services that can be critical to your success. Get to know the professionals in your area so that when you have a question, you can get it answered.

- Attorneys who specialize in real-estate transactions can help you draft an offer to purchase commercial properties and follow up with lease agreements for your tenants.

- A tax professional can offer important advice to help you structure you investments.

Commercial properties can be lucrative, but they are riskier and require more funds than investing in a single-family home you intend to rent or resell.

You can be successful if you research the market, know the laws associated with the type of property you are interested in pursuing, and move carefully to acquire it.

Finding your niche is what it's all about, isn't it?

You'll be more successful in your investment career if you genuinely like what you are doing.

If you don't enjoy working with people, taking on landlord duties probably isn't for you.

You can still own rentals, but plan on having someone else handle the management.

If you can't deal with stress, don't take on commercial properties or any property that seems extremely risky — at least not until you have plenty of extra cash and confidence in your ability to deal with all phases of a project.

Many investors start out by living in an investment property while they get it ready to sell or rent. That technique offers benefits, including the lower down-payment and interest rate that are available for owner-occupied dwellings, as well as one less mortgage payment.

Your Available Time

How much time do you have to devote to real estate?

The best profits are sometimes the result of refurbishing a cosmetically challenged or true fixer-upper property.

The more work you can do yourself, the more money will stay in your pocket when it's time to rent or sell.

However, if you already work sixty hours a week, you'll have to hire someone to handle every renovation task. That doesn't just lower profits — it often means it will take longer to complete the project.

Your Personal Life

Do you have a spouse, a family, or a significant other?

How do they feel about sharing you with your real-estate career?

A successful career in real estate takes a great deal of time and effort.

Once you've made it to some degree, you can delegate responsibilities and hire help, but for most of us that takes awhile. It's easier on your home life if your loved ones are interested in being involved in some way — or are at least understanding of your goals.

Your Hands-On Expectations

You're going to get your hands dirty. At the very least, plan on doing a lot of cleaning. Painting is a given, too.

How about laying tile and carpeting and taping off drywall — are you up to those chores?

If not, it will limit the number of properties you should consider, unless you have someone who will do the work for you for a reasonable fee.

Your Flair for Interior and Exterior Decor

You might be surprised how many buyers can't see past dirty floors and scuffed walls.

If you want to be successful in real-estate investing, you should be able to look beyond the surface and visualize what the structure will look like with a basic cleanup, then take it a step further to determine what kinds of changes would make significant improvements in its appearance and usability.

An effective way to train yourself to be able to see the potential in any property is to read decorating magazines, watch home-improvement shows, and browse the Internet for decorating ideas.

The more information you're exposed to, the more likely you are to instinctively know what should be done to make immediate improvements to a property, inside and out.

Where Will You Get the Funding?

Do you have savings or access to other funds?

Mortgage terms for investment properties aren't as liberal as loans for owner-occupied dwellings, and they're even stricter for commercial investments.

You might be able to persuade a seller to finance all or a portion of the property, but you'll need cash or a line of credit to make updates and repairs.

It might be worthwhile to float expenses for projects you think you can turn over quickly on a credit card, but you sure don't want to be stuck with a high-interest debt for very long. High credit-card balances can also affect the way mortgage lenders analyze your credit reports and scores.

How long can you handle a negative cash flow before it hurts you financially?

Your first project could go quickly, but it's more realistic to expect delays. Dealing with real-estate sales and rentals is a learning process, and it might take one or two transactions before your skills are consistent.

Plan your budget to include available cash for delays and possible setbacks.

Your Comfort Level

Most importantly, consider your comfort level.

How much are you willing to risk?

While it's true that real-estate investing is far less risky than the stock market or most business investments, the risk factors depend on what kind of real estate you're working with.

Investing in residential real estate carries less risk than commercial properties and land purchases, but some risk is still involved.

If you cannot deal with any type of risk at all, real estate is not your best investment choice.

Are you willing to make sacrifices?

Buying an investment property will probably take a bite out of your free money, the dollars you use to have fun. Are you willing to give that up for awhile?

Fewer dinners out, fewer vacations, a general cutback on entertainment — is it worth it to you to eliminate these things while you build equity in properties?

Analyze Your Real-Estate Market

There are potential real-estate investments of every type, from single-family residences to large commercial developments.

What's right for you?

Some investors are content buying and selling residential properties.

There's plenty of diversification in that single field because we can specialize in foreclosures, fixer-uppers, multifamily projects, or other types of residences. Every other area of real estate offers just as much variety, so there's something for everyone.

The trick is finding the segment of the real-estate market that you enjoy the most.

What's in Demand Close to Home?

Unless you live in a very small town, there are probably many real-estate investment avenues to pursue.

The most important thing you can do is keep your mind open to all possibilities. Look at properties from a fresh perspective, visualizing what they could be with updates or simple changes rather than focusing on their current conditions.

Most properties that are for sale are listed with real-estate agencies, so the majority of buyers go to agents when they are in the market to buy. Experienced real-estate agents can be one of your best sources of information about what buyers and renters are looking for.

Develop a relationship with one or more agents who specialize in the types of properties you want to buy.

Read all of your local papers, and pick up every real-estate for-sale publication that's available in your community.

Pay close attention to ads, noting prices versus features for rental homes and properties listed for sale.

Take regular drives through the communities you are most interested in.

Your goal is to become familiar with every aspect of the real-estate market in your town.

Chapter 4. Rental Properties

Most people want to become investors.

They want to be able to get rid of their debts, go on vacation when they would like, and make a lot of money in the process. Maybe they are tired of missing out on a lot of the important things in life, or they are tired of working for a boss who never seems to appreciate them the way that they should.

When they decide that it is time to work on a path to get out of their regular jobs, they may look to see what kinds of investments are out there for them to choose. And the good news is, there are actually quite a few that they are able to choose from.

From retirement to the stock market to starting your own business, there are choices that are going to work well for you. But with that said, when you want to have a lot of variety and a lot of fun with your investment, and you want to make a lot of money, either in the long term or the short term, then real estate investing is the right choice.

With flipping homes, you are going to have a short-term strategy. Your job is to purchase a property, get it fixed up, and then sell it quickly to make a big profit. With rental properties, you will get a property for a low price, and then move some tenants in there who will pay the mortgage, and a bit extra for your profits each month in order to see the returns on investing.

Both of these can be great options that will help you to make a lot of money in the real estate world. But they are quite a bit different. The strategies that you use with flipping homes is not going to be the same ones that you will use with rental properties at all, and it is important to keep these in mind.

While some investors like to expand out their portfolio a bit and have a combination of both of these going at the same time to diversify and bring in more profits, many beginners are just going to start with one or the other and become familiar with this.

For a beginner, one property at a time is usually a lot to handle, but it can be a great learning experience. You can always expand out and try the other method later on once you are pretty comfortable with the first one that you choose.

Since flipping homes and rental properties are going to be two different ways of investing in real estate, and they are going to be completely different, it is important to understand how each one works. Let's take a look at how each of these works, and why they are so important in this chapter.

Flipping Homes

First, we will look at the idea of flipping homes.

When you are flipping the home, your goal is to find a nice property that is undervalued for some reason, purchase it, and then fix it up as quickly as possible. Remember that the goal here is to get it done and sold as fast as you can so that you can take home a large profit, without being stuck paying the mortgage from one month to another.

When you get into the market of flipping homes, you want to find a property that is in need of some love and care. There should be some reason that others are not interested in the property. But when you walk in, you know that with a bit of work and a bit more money than the asking price, you will be able to fix it up and earn a lot of money in the process.

So, let's say that you are doing some research on properties in the area, and you see that there is a property that is being sold for $75,000. The other properties in that area often go for $150,000 to $175,000 so this seems like a property that may be worth your time. You go in and see that there needs to be a little bit of work that should be done on it and you that your costs to fix it up will be about $30,000.

While that amount will be a hefty sum, altogether you will spend just $105,000 on that property. You can then turn around and list it for $155,000 and if you sell it quickly, you will earn a profit of $55,000. However, if you go in and find that the property is listed for the $75,000, but it is going to take $100,000 to fix it up, then this is not worth your time. That is putting you at the very high end of the housing costs in that area, and it is not going to make you a profit, even if you do sell it for that high.

There are a few things that you need to consider when flipping a property.

- You need to know how much properties in that area are going for.

- You need to know how much the property is selling for.

- You need to know how much it will cost you to get the necessary fixes done to improve the value of the property.

- And you need to know how much you will need to spend on the closing fees, the mortgage for the time you hold onto the property (through the construction and the time it takes to sell the property), and any other costs and fees that come up.

- If you find the property and you know that you can get the fixes done fast and under budget, and you know the market is doing well and the property can sell within a few months, then this is the right property to go with and you should jump on it. But if you think the cost of the property is too much for that area, or the fixes will take up too much of the potential profits, then it is time to walk away and pick something else.

With these properties, when you are fixing things up remember that you need to spend a bit more money on them than you would do in a rental property.

With a rental property, the tenants want something nice, but they understand that the landlord is going for a lot of durabilities as well so laminate flooring and other cheaper fixes are fine in there.

But when you are looking at a house flip, you will need to put in nicer things. Some buyers want to imagine themselves living in this property for ten or more years, and they want it to be nice, which means that you will need to spend a bit more money.

Before you go out and purchase anything though, take some time to look up and research the things that buyers are paying more for in homes and your area. This can help you to spend your budget on the things that really need to be done.

Rental Properties

The other method of investing in real estate that you can choose to go with is rental properties. With the above option, you are trying to move quickly on a property and make a big lump sum of money in a short amount of time. But with a rental property, you are looking to the long term. You are interested in making a nice steady profit each month, and getting the tenant to pay off the mortgage and help you earn equity each month as well.

Starting out with a rental property is going to be similar to what you do with a house flip. You want to make sure that you pick out a property that is lower in price, especially for that area, and one that you will be able to fix up well without spending a lot of money. When you find a property that is low in price and can be fixed quickly, you purchase it and then start looking for tenants.

Your goal here is not to just sell the property as quickly as possible. Your goal is to go through and find someone willing to move into the property and pay you a rent each month.

If you got the repairs and the property for low enough, and the rent average in that area is high enough, you will be able to cover your mortgage, insurance, taxes, and the cost of repairs, while still making at least a small amount of profits each month.

The goal here is to make your tenants as happy as possible, and to pick out good tenants.

The happier the tenants are, and the more regular they are with your properties, the longer they will stay there and the steadier income you will be able to bring in each month.

The neat thing that comes with rental properties is that you also have the ability to sell them over time.

If you decide that you don't want to take care of a property after some time, or you decide to get out of investing in the rental property, you can then sell the property. Thanks to the work that you did with it, and the idea of appreciation, you will find that you can sell the property for a good profit as well.

So, with rental properties, not only are you able to make an income each month from the rent that your tenant pays, but you will also be able to make a big lump sum at the end of it all when you sell the property

Rental Properties Versus Flipping Homes

Now that we have taken the time to look at rental properties and fixing homes, you may be wondering which one you should choose to go with in order to bring in the profits that you are looking for.

Both of these can be so great for helping you to invest your money and make a good return. But some people find that one is better than the other for them. So, to help you make your decision, let's do a little comparison.

First, we are going to take a look at flipping homes. There are a lot of great benefits that come with flipping homes and taking in one lump sum of profit over the short term, rather than a smaller monthly payment over the short term. Some of the benefits that come with flipping homes include:

1. You can help out the local community because you take some of the properties in it that are run down and not looking as nice, and turn them over so they look amazing.
2. Can make you feel really accomplished that you sold a property and made a good profit in a short amount of time.
3. Leaves a lot of room for you to be creative.
4. You can use it as a way to be your own boss.
5. This investment source is going to be exciting, and allows you to be involved and hands-on with it as well.
6. If you do it right and can get the fixes done quickly, and find a good buyer, you will be able to make a good amount of profit in a short amount of time.

However, there are a few negatives that come with choosing to flip homes as your investment choice. These shouldn't be used to discourage you from jumping on the opportunity if you think it is the right one for you, but it is still good to understand some of the cons of this investment type so you can make the best decision for your needs. Some of the negatives with flipping homes, and the reason that not everyone decides to do it include:

1. There is a higher amount of risk.
2. There are holding costs, and sometimes it is difficult to sell the property when you are done.
3. Flipping homes can be really stressful and can cause anxiety.
4. Higher taxes on the profits that you make after flipping the home.
5. When you are ready to flip the home and save some money in the process, there is going to be a lot of manual labor and work on your part.

6. If you are not careful with your numbers, or you hold onto a property for too long, you could end up losing out on money rather than making a profit.

Now that we know a little bit more about the benefits and negatives of investing in flipping homes, it is time to move on to the idea of rental properties. There are a lot of investors who choose to go with rental properties in order to make a long-term profit on their investment. As with flipping homes, there are some positives and negatives to this form of investment. The positives of using rental properties will include:

1. You won't have to pay as much taxes on the profits you make from being a landlord.
2. You will usually have less construction and rehab to do on these properties because renters are not going to expect as much as buyers.
3. There is the possibility of long-term capital appreciation on the property, which can help you later on.
4. This can provide you with a passive income and cash flow that will last for the long term.

While these benefits can be really nice to have, and will entice a lot of investors to really choose to work with the rental properties rather than flipping homes (or even some of the other investment options that are out there), there are a few things that you need to pay attention to, and a few negatives, that come with investing in these rental properties. Some of the negatives that can come with investing in rental properties include:

1. You have to be the one who properly maintains the rental property until you decide to sell it.

2. You will need to have more than one rental property, with low vacancies, in order to turn this into an income that you can live on.

3. You may have to deal with a lot of bad tenants if you are not careful. This can lead to problems with them not paying rent, damage to the property, and even having to go through the property of evicting the tenant if things get bad enough.

4. You have to be an active manager with these properties.

How to Begin Rehabbing Houses?

To get started with rehabbing houses, the first thing every investor should do is study their market area, look into the financing alternatives available, and put together a team to carry out your task with. To get the ball rolling, you can be part of a real estate networking program in your neighborhood. This way, you can meet and get to know other professionals in the real estate industry. In addition to meeting other real estate investors, if you are a newbie in this field, you can also get to meet mentors that will help you make the right decisions. While you get more conversant with what is involved in rehabbing a house, you can begin by looking for the right properties.

Steps in Rehabbing a House

- Get a professional inspector to help you in evaluating the property.

- Come up with a checklist which will help you rehab the house from beginning to end in an organized form.

- As soon as you can have an understanding of all the work that will be done, come up with a budget.

- Locate a contractor that has the qualifications to carry out your rehab plans.

- Get the permits that are needed to get your project started.

- Get started with demolition and cleanup for the renovations to start.

- Begin carrying out improvements on the exterior that will make the property have an excellent appeal.

- Make interior improvements a priority by selecting repairs which will help you get the best out of every investment.

- Ensure every improvement is finalized before ending with the project.

Investors should also consider making an offer. In this introductory phase, real estate investors are required to look into the amount involved with a deal. This way, they can assess the exact kind of offer they are to make.

What's more, the after repair value (**ARV**) gauge, which plays a major role in the calculation of the property's value after repairs will also be involved. This number is essential and will help investors come up with financing alternatives which are ideal for the situation they are in and also have the right exit strategy.

Chapter 5. The Cycle of Wealth

Building Your Business Channel

If you plan to travel from New York City to San Francisco, you will see good road signs that will guide you to find your way without using a comprehensive road map that describes your journey.

The same applies when you decide to invest in the business. If you have a clear picture of the benefits and advantages of different kinds of real estate deals, assessing your current position in terms of resources, as well as moving in the right direction with the least amount of wasted time, it will be a major asset to you. This is the focus of this chapter—to help you start to see where you are, where you want to go, and the right way to get there.

The first thing you need to do is to your financial evaluation at this moment in time. Is your credit strong or weak?

Do you have access to money lending avenues? Are private and public lenders ready to help you get started? Once you have clearly examined your current status, you are okay to start selecting the right kind of deals to push you towards financial freedom.

For instance, if you have smaller credit resources, you will want to select real estate deals that do not depend on either credit or funding.

One of these deals is "wholesaling."

Hence, let's start this by exploring the different methods to make money, as well as the type of money needed to accomplish that kind of deal.

Property Types and Investment Approaches

Real estate investing is a great investment because of the many property types that one can invest in, plus techniques for what to do with those properties. And each has its own rewards.

Investors factor different options depending on the result they want to accomplish, the amount of money they want to invest in the project, and their level of experience with various strategies.

For instance, an investor might want to go for quick cash investment methods for different reasons, among them lack of enough capital to work with, or high consumer debt.

Multiple income channels and opportunities demand the right knowledge to specialize in different parts.

Multiple Income Streams

You could be wondering how to select your streams of income and what factors should dictate your decision.

Here's a list of the **different types of income**:

- ✓ Wholesaling
- ✓ Probate
- ✓ Remodeling
- ✓ Rehabbing
- ✓ Land development
- ✓ Discount note selling
- ✓ Foreclosures

Meanwhile, here are some **passive streams of income in real estate**:

- ✓ Leases
- ✓ Property management
- ✓ Recreational parks
- ✓ Rentals
- ✓ Apartment houses
- ✓ Mobile home parks

In general, anything that you will contract and sell quickly falls into earned income.

Passive income refers to money that you get week after week, or monthly without you going out and doing another deal. As a result, passive income is sometimes called a recurring income.

When it comes to real estate, properties that fall under passive streams of income are your buy and hold rentals. Once you close on these deals, you collect rent every single month.

Another real estate field that can be considered passive is when you become a property manager, or you own a property management company, and investors use you to collect the rents for them and pay you some fee for doing it.

Portfolio Income

Here is when your money starts to generate money for you, especially through interest.

There are different ways to generate portfolio income that is real estate related. Most of these methods of income relate to the investor earning interest on his or her money. While this will not dig much into these methods, it is critical for you to understand the definition of these income streams.

Types of Portfolio Streams of Income in Real Estate

Real estate can help investors build wealth through a systematic channel that builds upon itself.

While everyone is different with different demands and goals on their time, professional real estate investors will always want to between 3-5 streams of earned income, and 2-3 streams of portfolio income.

New investors that have a limited amount of money start by being knowledgeable in various earned income streams like foreclosure, wholesale, and rehabbing. Now, they have a lot of freedom over their potential to generate huge amounts of cash in a short period of time. Next, they take that money and begin to invest in buy and hold properties.

As the passive income increases or the lease option properties grows, the investor has two choices to make: either purchase another buy and hold property or invest in a portfolio stream.

Distressed Properties vs. Motivated Sellers

There is an old saying about real estate investing that goes, "There are only two types of deals out there, distressed properties or distressed sellers."

No matter your investment strategy, you will realize that certain properties have a higher ideal investment opportunity than others.

Professional investors compare each deal against a set of merits and consider the benefits of that type of deal versus the opportunities present. They don't always fulfill each characteristic defined, but they assess and make informed decisions.

When evaluating a distressed property, look for the following advantages:

- There is minimal competition for them because the average individual wants properties in the best condition.
- You can always buy distressed properties under flexible, easy terms and for prices relatively below the market value.
- You have the freedom to heighten the value through smaller improvements and rehab work.
- A lot of market areas have many distressed properties to select from.
- Some things to consider about distressed properties include:
- Many real estate markets have a certain number of investors searching for this type of properties, so your marketing efforts

should be active, well-organized, and effective to discover better deals. It can be great to investigate different marketing strategies that have done well for other real estate investors.

- In order to avoid costly mistakes, you must know how to examine the property and its neighborhood accurately.

- Through inspections and repairs, estimates have to be done before the purchase.

- If the property is located in a lower-income neighborhood, the comparable sales in that particular place will surpass a specific amount of money, regardless of how change is done. Repairs are usually costly. In order to optimize profitability in the older, lower-income areas, it is safe to integrate a distressed property with a distressed seller and take advantage of the profit potential on every aspect.

Meanwhile, here are the pros of working with distressed sellers:

- There is seller distress in each price range.

- Sometimes, you can buy properties under flexible and easy terms. The seller requires help, and in most cases, just wants a way out, but does not know what to do. You can offer a solution.

- Seller distress often results from property distress, so the opportunities of being able to increase property value through cosmetic changes or rehabbing when you can connect a distressed seller with a distressed property are great.

- You must know what caused the seller to experience the situation they are in and find out the best way to help them get out of it. To understand their problem and find the best solution, you must develop good listening and negotiation skills.

- Certain distressed sellers give compelling reasons why they want to remain in their properties, and the tendency is to want to accommodate this. If their problem is for financial reasons, this can be risky. It is relevant to keep your emotions out of it.

Purchasing as Wholesale

Distressed properties are the best option for wholesaling candidates. And wholesaling is a great opportunity because it requires the least expertise and is the kind of deal new investors want.

Wholesale deals might be one of the first types of deals you will make in real estate investing because you stand a great chance to land distressed properties.

In order to succeed with wholesaling, some of the things that you need to know do include how to segment your market correctly, how to create a database of possible properties, and many more. Also, you need to understand a few basic elements of the wholesaling business, including:

Analyzing Prospects

Because distressed properties should be your main target, you must learn how to identify and distressed homes. You also need to understand that a distressed property doesn't imply that a deal is good, but that it is a great start. So you need to memorize the techniques to help you know when a deal is too good to be true, when it is the right time to move forward, and when the deal needs to be left on the table.

Computing the Market Value

You must know the significance of calculating fair market value after repairs to succeed as a wholesaler. The real estate experts on your power team will be a valuable asset for finding this information. Also, by using comparable sales of properties in the same location will allow you to know the market value.

Estimating Repairs

This will not be a successful process if you fail to approximate repairs correctly. Learn how to check deals to make sure you present an offer that will lead to the highest profit. There are also techniques you can learn that will save you cash on rehab projects and optimize your profits.

Submitting Offers and Counter-Offers

You have to become familiar with good communication and negotiating skills, learn how to submit offers and counteroffers without destroying your goals, and learn how to manage contracts. Understanding how to properly properties will be significant in determining what to offer and whether you need to make an offer.

Getting Buyers

Wholesaling is half-done when you can find deals and bargain, but there is no one to assign contracts to. Creating a sizable investor database to tap no matter the kind of deal you are working on will assist you in moving things forward quickly and maintain your profit margins.

How to Close Effectively

It is important you learn the right ways to close without money.

Look at local demographics. Is your buyer pool made up primarily of one group of people, such as senior citizens? Knowing as much as you can about the population makeup will help you with any type of real-estate investment, from selling single-family homes to finding commercial tenants that specialize in businesses and services important to your town.

National and International Opportunities

If you can't find what you're looking for locally, branch out to other areas. There's never been a better time to shop nationally or internationally — the Internet brings distant real-estate opportunities to anyone who has a computer and a Web connection.

Let's say your market research shows that senior citizens make up a large portion of the buying pool in your town. They likely want a house that's not too small, but not too large, either. A three-bedroom, two-bath home is perfect, something around 2,000 square feet or slightly less.

Local agents have advised you to look for a house with no steps — or just a few. Even seniors who aren't bothered by steps yet are looking for one-level living with a minimum of stairs to climb. That eliminates split-foyer homes, homes where you must climb high porches in order to enter the front door, and homes with finished living areas on two levels.

Most seniors want a house in move-in condition. They don't want to paint or make repairs. That's where you step in. Your goal is to find a house that's structurally sound and has the required features but that needs cosmetic updates. If you can't find that type of house at a bargain price, you might need to look at houses that need a little more work, but for this first purchase, steer clear of anything that involves structural repairs unless you are an experienced builder.

A downside of distant investments is managing them effectively, so be prepared to hire someone to handle tenants and maintenance for you. The extra expense must be considered when you analyze the potential returns on your investment.

But before you branch out to other areas, it's important to become accustomed to your local real-estate market. Real-estate transactions are handled very differently across the United States. Worldwide, you'll see even more variations. Understanding your local process will give you more confidence and better prepare you to ask questions about the procedures in other areas.

One way to begin a real-estate investment career at a distant location is to buy a vacation home. How about an area where you like to spend a few weeks each year, or a location where you think you would like to retire? Chances are it's a spot you already know at least a little bit about, and that can be a plus when it's time to select properties.

If you have a child or grandchild away from home in college, consider buying a house or condo instead of paying rent for a dorm or apartment. The residence will fill a need during the young person's college years, and its value will appreciate for you. Make the time away from home an investment opportunity instead of paying rent for four or more years. Sell the home when your child leaves school, or continue to use it as a rental for other students.

Finding Your First Investment

Buying a single-family home is a great way to start your real-estate investment career. Why should you go with a single-family residence? Because they are generally the properties in most demand, which in turn makes them the easiest properties to sell. Let's walk through a typical scenario, in which you've researched the market in preparation to buy a single-family home.

Let's say your market research shows that senior citizens make up a large portion of the buying pool in your town. They likely want a house that's not too small, but not too large, either. A three-bedroom, two-bath home is perfect, something around 2,000 square feet or slightly less.

Local agents have advised you to look for a house with no steps — or just a few. Even seniors who aren't bothered by steps yet are looking for one-level living with a minimum of stairs to climb. That eliminates split-foyer homes, homes where you must climb high porches in order to enter the front door, and homes with finished living areas on two levels.

Most seniors want a house in move-in condition. They don't want to paint or make repairs. That's where you step in. Your goal is to find a house that's structurally sound and has the required features but that needs cosmetic updates. If you can't find that type of house at a bargain price, you might need to look at houses that need a little more work, but for this first purchase, steer clear of anything that involves structural repairs unless you are an experienced builder.

Lease Options

The lease is one of the most interesting real estate investment opportunities for both new and experienced investors because they can produce multiple income streams within a single deal. Here are some general points you need to know about lease options in real estate: if you purchase a property using a lease option, you can:

- Interact with distressed sellers and not distressed properties. Circumstances of the seller create the deal. What you need to do is to identify the problem owners.

- Acquire freedom of a property without taking ownership. You are not mandated to buy, but you have attained the right to purchase.

- Manage nice homes in great places. In this case, the seller needs to get out, and the investor gets in. Better neighborhood increases demand.

- Help another person in different ways. The defining aspect of lease options is always debt relief. You are always working with people who might not want to sell their property, but who have to sell it because of financial issues. Thus, you can help someone find a solution quickly.

Similarly, you can do it with or without any money.

Foreclosures

The foreclosure market can be a great channel for making a profit both for new and experienced investors. Foreclosure happens every day, and this can be your chance not to grab a wise investment, but also help someone in need.

Keep in mind that foreclosures can happen for various reasons, and this is a niche where you can achieve a win-win scenario and do something that assists both you and the individual in need. Investors must be able to negotiate well with both lenders and homeowners to boost profits on these deals.

With multiple strategies to use and ways to generate money in real estate, knowledge will be a vital factor for you to succeed.

By the available opportunities in real estate investing, you will have completed your first critical step towards achieving financial independence. Now, is the time to proceed to the next level.

Chapter 6. Real Estate Market

Let's see how the investor can buy rental properties in different markets, ranging from rural markets to urban markets.

Rural Markets

If you are a future investor, you likely do not want to jump into the deep end of real estate investing by purchasing the most expensive condominium you can afford in downtown Manhattan, just to deal with a punishing mortgage for the next thirty years. It is in scenarios such as these that rural markets play an important role for the future mogul. Rural markets, as one would imagine, tend to be less expensive than downtown centers and urban markets.

However, this is not always the case. It really depends in the type of rural market. A hundred years ago, rich people owned properties in urban centers, such as New York and Chicago.

The poor, on the other hand, lived in the outskirts of the cities or in rural areas. Currently however, the roles are changing. While many wealthy people still live in urban regions, we are experiencing a change in their patterns, as some very wealthy investors are purchasing rural properties. This is especially true for commercial farms, private ranches, and large estates which may cost millions of dollars. While at first glance, the reader may be confused as to where to begin with rural markets, here is a neat trick: measure the distance of the markets to the nearest city.

There are a two main advantages and disadvantages to rural properties being less expensive than urban properties. First, as ly hinted, because they are less expensive, the startup cash is not as prohibitive. A major hurdle to first-time investors is collecting the startup cash to purchase your first property. The less expensive rural properties are a major draw for first-timers.

While there are clearly differences in price between rural and urban properties, there are other nuances that make rural properties a worthwhile investment. First is the difference in turnovers between rural and urban properties. The term turnover refers to the number of tenants that come in and out of your properties. Having a single renter in your property for fifteen years is a blessing in the real estate market. Dealing with changes in tenants on a bimonthly basis is painful and you will lose money with empty apartments along with the wear and tear on your properties.

Because rural areas are less populated, there are fewer similar apartments or homes for people to move to, meaning that you are less likely to experience severe turnover in your investments. This stability is great for cash flow purposes, meaning that you will be less likely to be paying the mortgage on empty apartments.

For the same reason that there is little turnover in rural areas, there is also less competition from other investors, meaning that while the pond may be smaller, you're the bigger fish. This is especially true with older rural properties. Not only do they sell for less money, there is also less competition for them. Along this vein, there is an important point to be made. Because rural real estate is less competitive, it is not such a cutthroat industry as urban real estate which resembles something closer to survival of the fittest.

Especially when looking at rural properties, it is important to note that there are huge differences in the types of investments you can make. Barns, farms, and ranches all have different challenges, but one thing holds them all together: they are plentiful in rural areas.

This solid supply of properties makes rural communities a viable place for the future mogul to invest their money. Here's another advantage to rural properties: low taxes. Nothing absolutely destroys your bottom line as having to pay upwards of 60% of your tenants' rents in property taxes. Because rural communities tend to tax less (fewer schools, less infrastructure, etc.), back-end costs to investing in these regions may pay dividends in the long run.

After all, taxes are a sunk cost - you cannot recuperate them and your benefits from them are indirect. Aligned with fewer property taxes, rural communities also tend to have less regulation. Since most people in rural communities are spread further apart than they are in urban sectors, it doesn't matter that much what they do in their own homes, leading to less overall regulation.

Before we discuss suburban and town real estate markets, it's important to contrast the differences between rural and urban markets. In this spirit, this work will now look at urban markets so the reader can compare the differences with the rural markets.

Urban Markets

The first thing to know about urban markets is that they are all extremely different. Just like in the game Monopoly, the differences between Mediterranean Avenue costing $60 and Boardwalk setting you back $400 are staggering. Unlike rural markets where an investor can clearly notice the differences between an expensive ranch and a run-down barn, these distinctions are blurred in urban markets. On top of this, each city in the United States has a slum and skyscrapers with million-dollar penthouses. The staggering differences between properties in urban markets can leave potential investors lost so here are some details that may smooth out the transition for the reader.

There is another advantage to investing in urban properties over rural ones. Urban properties are remarkably easy to resell. Because of the lower level competition in rural markets, there are fewer people vying for fewer properties, rendering such markets more difficult if the investor is looking for a fixer-upper or to turn properties quickly. Fixer-uppers, as the name suggests, are those often-foreclosed properties that an investor buys at a discount from a bank, fixes them up, and then resells them for a profit.

This style of real estate investing works much better in urban markets than in rural markets precisely because of the fast resale rates of urban markets. Put in economic terms, urban markets are more "liquid," meaning that they can be turned into cash on hand, than rural markets. It's important for the future mogul to know that this is a way to invest in the urban real estate market, if done correctly, for some serious profits.

Yet another advantage to the urban market is property appreciation. As a general rule of thumb, the investor should be wary of small percentages of appreciation in value in smaller cities. Investing in a shrinking economy is generally not a good idea, especially if this economy correlates with a shrinking population. Rural markets move on a much slower time scale, thereby appreciating at far gentler a rate than urban markets.

Suburban Markets

When investors talk about different real estate markets, they tend to simply differentiate between rural and urban regions, assuming that suburbs are simply the halfway point to both markets. This could not be further from the truth. Suburbans may as well be their own animal when it comes to real estate investing so this is dedicated to showing you how to differentiate between suburban properties and where the pros and cons are for this market. First and foremost, as an investor, the last situation you want is empty rooms with a mortgage. These scenarios force the investor to continue paying for the home, along with taxes and insurance, without tenants actually using the homes themselves and paying rent.

With this knowledge in mind, a unique and positive characteristic of the suburban real estate market is the slow turnover rate. The reader will recall that turnover is the changing of tenants over and over again. As an investor, this unreliability in renters creates more paperwork, leaves more to chance, leaves apartments empty, and leads to less stability.

All of these factors increase uncertainty and lead to less confidence in investing. Luckily, suburban markets are reliably stable. Tenants choosing to live in suburban markets tend to have small families, have stable jobs, can pay rent, and tend to save money. Because of this, they often prefer more permanent locations. When investing in suburban real estate markets, pay special attention to the school districts there, as many parents with young children will move to better school districts so that their children can have a better education than they would have elsewhere. If your property can attract these tenants, you will likely have renters in these properties for a long time. The downside to these more permanent tenants is that there may be a lack of interest in renting.

Most people who live in the suburbs are small families or those looking to have a family of their own in the future. This means that there may be an overall interest buying homes rather than renting them for long periods of time. However, as stated, if they have small kids, they may be interested in changing homes due to more competitive school districts in some neighborhoods over others.

Where the future investor can distinguish herself or herself is in knowing their clients and their needs. The real issue here is that those who live in the suburbs are accustomed to "owning" their possessions. They likely have their cars paid off, have their own furniture, and are generally more interested in owning a home as well.

Connected to owning a vehicle, there is additionally a general lack of public transportation in suburban parts of the United States. While it is nearly impossible to move in urban areas without public transportation, very few buses and subways reach suburban communities.

Connected to the permanence of the tenants in suburban markets is that they tend to treat your properties with greater care. Because of this, the appliances of the home tend to be taken care of at a better rate than in urban sectors where tenants may move from property to property with little care for the appliances. Since many children are living in these suburban properties, parents usually wish to teach them good cleaning and maintenance habits, leading these units to be a better "bang for your buck" as an investor. This respect for your property goes a long way in its resale value, especially if your tenants view your property as a home, rather than as a temporary living space.

General Concept of Real Estate

Real estate investing is a practice where a person will acquire a home or another property. That person could hold onto the property for an extended period of time.

In some cases, that investor has full rights to the property regarding what can be done with it. In other cases, the investor might have full control over the buildings and the land that the property entails thus adding to the assets that one has for use.

The general goal of real estate investing is to sell the property in the future at a profit. An investor will need to find a way to sell the property after its value increases. This could come from either the natural increase of the property's value or from any improvements that have been made to the property. Sometimes the value can increase when enough tenants use the property. This includes not only having enough renters but also having them remain as renters for a long while.

This is an exciting field that you can participate in with many types of properties. You could get this to work with a traditional home or from a commercial building that is used like an office building or shopping center. Whatever it is you find, you might get something exciting out of your investments.

Local market

Checking your local market is essential as there are many options to choose from no matter where you are. You could invest in real estate in any part of the world. Every part of the world has some kind of real estate that you could invest in. You just have to search to see what can be of use to you. Do you want a vacation home in Sri Lanka and rent it out to people who need a place to stay while in the area? Do you want to invest in a strip mall in Atlanta or some other city with a growing economy? It does not matter where the property is located.

You have the option to invest in anything so long as you check out what is available. You can always stay with your local market if you prefer, but having the option to find real estate in another corner of the world is always something worth thinking about. You have to be aware of the rules associated with investing in a property in another country. These include rules about what can be done with a property and the tax laws for that country, and even if you can own property as a foreign buyer. Details on choosing between a local or long-distance property will be covered later in this guide.

Long-Term needs

Real estate investing focuses on long-term needs. While many different investments are ones that could change quickly, real estate is something that increases in value over time. You might hold onto a property for several years before you actually sell it. It might take a while for you to sell a property, but it could be worthwhile when you actually get to that point. To understand this, you have to look at how a real estate transaction is different from a traditional stock purchase. Real estate requires research and analysis plus an extensive contract and maintenance to keep a property in the best shape possible or to find the right tenants.

It could take years for the property investment to be worthwhile when everything is considered. A regular stock purchase is very different. In this case, you would simply have to research a business and then execute a trade within a few minutes. You could then sell that stock in a few hours if you wish if you see that the price is rising. This simplicity of trading makes it possible to quickly acquire or trade it rather fast. This is not always the best thing in the world because the trading volume on something can be high.

An investment like this might change in value quickly. It is also easy for people to develop strong emotions when trading stocks; they might let their emotions cloud their common sense. With real estate, you will not have to worry about the value of your investment changing dramatically. The market has less liquidity, meaning that people cannot enter and leave it quickly. It takes a while for some properties to change in value.

This is a good thing as it gives you time to plan your strategy for investing and for deciding on ways to make your property more valuable and attractive to others.

The intricate and specific nature of the real estate market is also one that requires far more research and investigation than other fields. You have to spend a long time investigating which properties are right for your investment. It can take some time to find the right property, but the rewards will be great when you find one that you want to invest in.

Chapter 7. The Different Type Of Lease

In this, we are going to cover the different types of Lease Options.

Property-first Lease Option

A Property-first Lease Option is where you have a property, and you are trying to find a tenant buyer for it. There are many reasons why you would have a property first.

Maybe you have an investor who owns a property and wants to get rid of it. This investor is motivated. Perhaps you have a regular property owner who is trying to get rid of their property. This owner is motivated. Maybe you have an owner who is in a bad financial situation and is deciding to refinance their home to pay off their debt, but the banks won't let them. We could convert the owner into a Lease Option tenant buyer by buying their house. I call this a tenant owner property.

A tenant-owned property is still just a seller, but this seller is going to become your tenant once they sell the property to an investor. That's what I call a Lease-Buy-Back, which is just another variation of the property-first Lease Option.

The owners have gotten themselves into a financial situation and can't get out of it. We have to bring in an investor to purchase the property from the owner. The owner stays in the house and leases it back from us, thus becoming a tenant buyer. They enter into a Lease Option agreement

In summary, there are three types of property-first Lease Options: the seller owned, the investor-owned, and the tenant owned.

Another property-first Lease Option would be if you went out and bought a property yourself because you thought it was a good investment because it was really undervalued.

Tenant-first Lease Option

The next type of Lease Option is a "tenant-first" Lease Option. This is where you go out and find someone that can't qualify for a mortgage but wants to buy a house. They found you as a result of your various advertising efforts. I also get a lot of my tenant buyer leads from my mortgage brokers because they have people who were looking to get a mortgage, but they couldn't qualify them.

When we find a potential tenant buyer, the first thing we do is try to put them in one of the properties we already have in our listings. If they don't like any properties we already have, we go out, and we try to find a property from a motivated seller. It's relatively easy to pair up a motivated tenant buyer with a motivated seller.

Another way of finding a property in a tenant-first strategy is to purchase a property for them. As mentioned, the way we do that is through an investor or by purchasing it ourselves. Either of these options would be our last course of action. I would probably assign the deal to another Lease Option expert before I would purchase a property myself.

Sandwich Lease Option

The third type of Lease Option is what is commonly known as a Sandwich Lease Option. This is where we lease a property from a motivated seller, and then we sublet it to a tenant buyer. We sandwich ourselves in the middle of the deal. Really, it's just another variation of the property-first strategy.

In the following , we will cover the three types of Lease Options in more detail

2.1 Property-First Lease Option

A property-first Lease Option is when we have a property, and we are trying to find a tenant buyer to put in that property. The reason we would have a property-first is:

1.Seller owned. A motivated seller has a house that they haven't been able to sell. They had to move for a new job, or they purchased another home or many other reasons. They are motivated because they now have two mortgage payments, and they can no longer afford these payments. They are very motivated to sell.

2.Investor owned. An investor owns an investment property, and they are having a hard time managing the property. They have had bad tenants, and they are just fed up with being a landlord. They want out! "Just take my property." They are very motivated.

3. Tenant owned. A tenant owned property is where the owner has run up a bunch of credit and can no longer afford all their monthly expenses. Their housing expenses, their credit cards, and all those expenses that make up their monthly payments have gotten out of control. They have to sell their home or lose it. They are usually close to foreclosure. They are very desperate, but they do not want to move. They like the neighborhood; their kids are enrolled in school there. So, we bring in an investor, and we purchase the property from the existing owner, and the owner then becomes the tenant.

4. Company Purchase. I like a property, and I go out and purchase that property at a much reduced price.

Now that we have the property, we have to find the tenant. We have to make sure that we market that property appropriately to the right target market. You will want to use many different marketing channels such as online classifieds, social media, Youtube, etc. We must find a tenant for that property reasonably quick, or we may lose the opportunity.

You also want to be doing ongoing marketing to build up a database of tenant buyers. While it may be called property-first, it may be that you already have lots of potential tenant buyers that you are working with who are interested in a Lease Option.

Again, a Property-First Lease Option is when you have the property, and you are trying to find a tenant buyer for that property.

2.2 Tenant-First Lease Options

Some people would argue that Tenant-First Lease Options are much easier to do. My experience is that they are more challenging to do. First of all, you have to find the tenant buyer, and you have to qualify that person, and then you have to find a property that they like. Then you have to purchase that property or convince a motivated seller to do a Lease Option with you.

The first thing we do when looking for tenant buyers is we advertise on our different channels. We advertise in online classified ads, online 'For Sale by Owner' sites, on Twitter, on Facebook, on YouTube, etc. The other place where we find tenant buyers is through mortgage brokers and Realtors.

Potential tenant buyers are people that are trying to purchase a home, and when they apply for a mortgage discover that they can't get qualified. So now they are stuck. The purchasers are all excited because they thought they were going to purchase this property, and now they find out they can't. This is where we come in.

What we do in this case is we bring in an investor and buy that property for them. We work out a Lease Option arrangement whereby we lease the property back to people who couldn't qualify. It's not always the case that we have investors available. In that situation, we have to go searching for the right investor.

There are several things we do to find a qualified tenant buyer for a Lease Option.

First, we run our marketing to try and locate a tenant buyer. Then we do some pre-qualifying upfront. That usually means asking for a down payment and finding out what their income is. We need to know how much money they make so that when they go out looking for properties, they can find a property that is in their price range.

There have been many times where we have shopped around for a property with the tenant buyer, and then find out they don't have the deposit like they said they had. There have been a few occasions where these people said they had their minimum deposit, which was $10,000, and we go out shopping with them, and it turns out they don't have the $10,000. Then they ask us if we have some program where they could pay for their deposit in installments. I have tried doing installment plans in the past, and I have gotten burnt just about every time. I will never do that again.

You have to make sure that you pre-qualify the tenant buyer before you go shopping for houses with them. When we look at their income, we also look at the Gross Debt Service (GDS) ratio and the Total Debt Service (TDS) ratio to determine how much of a home that they can afford.

The GDS and TDS are calculations that help determine how much lease payment they can afford based on their income debt (e.g., credit cards, car payments, etc.).

The tenant-first Lease Option strategy is about trying to find a qualified tenant that meets our criteria. A qualified tenant buyer means that they have the deposit and that they have enough income to cover their current debt payments.

Since the banks didn't approve these prospects, their credit score will be bad, or they didn't have enough down payment or both. We understand this when going into the deal. That's the nature of the Lease Option business. We know they are not the perfect loan candidates; otherwise, they wouldn't be coming to us.

Now that we have the tenant buyer, the next step is to go looking for a property for them. The first thing we try to do is show them one of the properties that we have available from a motivated seller or a motivated investor.

If they don't like any of these, then we go out, and we look for other properties from other motivated sellers. Finally, if that doesn't work, then we look for investors to buy a property that meets the tenant buyer's specific needs.

Once we acquire a property, we put the contracts in place. There is no difference between the contracts that we use with the tenant-first arrangement and the contracts that we use for the property-first arrangement. It's the upfront work that we have to do that is different between these two types of Lease Option strategies.

2.3 Sandwich Lease Option

A Sandwich Lease Option is where you, as the Lease Option broker, are sandwiched between the homeowner and the tenant buyer.

What that means is there is a contractual relationship between you and the seller as well as between you and the buyer. There are two contracts. There are a Lease Agreement and an Option Agreement between you and the seller.

The Lease Agreement between you and the seller would determine the lease payment to the seller, the term of the lease and the responsibilities of each party.

So, for example, let's say your agreement with the seller is for $1,000 a month. You are leasing the property from the seller for $1,000 a month for three years, and you will take care of all maintenance and repairs.

Next, the Option Agreement between you and the seller would determine the Option Price, the term of the agreement, and how the credits are to be applied.

For example, let's say that you have the right to purchase that property from the seller for $200,000. You would have an Option Agreement with the seller for $200,000, with $300 a month credits applied toward the down payment.

You have similar agreements with the tenant buyer. You have a Lease Agreement with the tenant buyer but for a higher amount. You always want to make sure that the amount that you are charging the tenant buyer is higher than what you have to pay the seller. Otherwise, you have a negative cash flow.

In this example, let's say that you have an arrangement with the tenant buyer that you're going to collect from them $1,200 a month. That means you would have a $200 spread between what you are charging the tenant buyer and what you're paying the seller. That positive cash flow is essential in real estate investing. It's especially important when you're doing Lease Options.

The other contract that you have with the tenant buyer is the Option Agreement, which specifies that the tenant buyer has the right to buy the property from you for another amount. In this case, let's say it is 220,000. If you recall, you have the right to purchase the property from the current owner for $200,000. And since the tenant buyer has the right to buy the property from you for $220,000, that's a $20,000 profit spread.

So you sandwich yourself in the middle of this whole lease option process, thus the name, "sandwich Lease Option." It's a lot more complicated when it comes time for closing because now you have four contracts. The bank doesn't want to see all these contracts. They only want to see the agreement of purchase and sale between the two parties: the seller and the buyer.

To finalize a Sandwich Lease Option, you would have to assign the contracts. Make sure the people you assign the contracts to know how to execute them at the end of the term.

So, at the end of the term, you can either assign your Lease Option agreement that you have with the tenant buyer to the seller, and they can execute it that way. Or you can even assign the Lease Option contract you have with the seller to the tenant buyer. An assignment is very complicated, and I won't go into all the details here. A good lawyer will need to be involved. Just keep in mind that you are sandwiched between the two parties.

Another way you arrange this is to have a joint venture agreement and a management agreement with the owner, and they have an option agreement directly with the tenant buyer. This arrangement avoids the issue of the tenant having an option agreement with you when you don't own the property. Optioning out a property that you don't own has become a legal issue with some of the transactions I have seen.

Chapter 8. What Are Good Investment

Strategies

Now that you have read about the steps you need to take before you invest in real estate, this will outline good investment strategies that will help you to begin real estate investing.

Start Small

Investors who have had a good amount of success began small. They buy one property to start. Before they purchased, they researched the area where they decided they wanted to invest. The ideals that make a good location to invest in –shopping convenience, schools, adjacency to major highways/freeways, businesses that provide services to the residents in the area. There is information from a number of sources that can provide the data you can use to get all the information needed.

Here are some websites that give investors the information they need to make educated decisions about an area where they want to invest

Zillow– Local Market Report – This is a free site that publishes sales data, as well as rental information on a national basis. Properties that are for sale that are listed on the Multiple Listing Service (MLS) are also listed on Zillow. You can get property information by entering an address, or if you want information about a specific area, you can enter a city name or zip code. This report gives information comparing the property you are interested in with other properties in the surrounding area that are either being currently on the market for sale or homes that are rental and the rate of rent being paid in the area.

Multiple Listing Service (MLS) – This site has the most updated listing information and is exclusive to licensed real estate professionals. The information revises throughout the day and evening based on information entered or deleted from the site. Reports from this site can be printed by local real estate associations and make the data available on their own website. (Carson, 2014)

Investment Location

The property you plan to invest in needs to be in a good location. This is probably the most important part of real estate investing. Finances and employment are other essentials that need to be part of the research to find areas that demonstrate they are stable and profitable.

Affordability, population growth, and job growth are three considerations that will influence your decision where the best places are for investing and creating positive cash flow. (Fettke, 2016)

If you do research and find that there is a property in an area that is affordable, has what appears to be population growth, and the Sears store in the mall will be closing their door in four months, what do you think the viability of having a profitable property as a rental will be?

The answer is a slim probable to not at all. If a business that is a major employer leaves an area, a domino effect follows. The employed lose their jobs. Along with their jobs being lost, they may have to move out of the area to get work elsewhere. That means there will be more properties available, some that will probably be other rentals but no renters to rent them to. Along with the major employer closing, other smaller businesses in the area will lose money and may have to close as well. Restaurants that were frequented lose lunch and dinner crowd customers because people who are not working don't have the extra money to dine out. It affects everything in the area.

What was an affordable neighborhood that had job growth loses job growth when there is sufficient job loss? The loss of a business that has a financial impact on an area changes the face of a neighborhood. It doesn't mean the people change it, it changes the people and what they need to do to find future employment. Unless another similar type of business moves into the area giving the area opportunities for employment, investing in the area is not a wise decision.

The questions you need to ask when you begin to do your research of an area are what the industries and businesses are located in the area? Are there shopping malls, mom and pop businesses, banks, restaurants, hi-tech companies?

Are the industries diverse or is there one major industry? Are they stable? Is there a military base or college campus?

Are there new businesses or corporations being built in the area? Any key improvements to the community – a new mall or additional stores to an existent mall, a Target or a Walmart, Starbucks, restaurants?

Are salaries stable, increasing or decreasing? How can I find out about what the median salaries are? Is there a stable employment climate or are there layoffs that will be coming in the near future?

There isn't an area that is 100% perfect. However, if there is a solid combination of varied industries, a low unemployment rate, and stable median salaries, then if you find something that resonates a positive outlook, this is as close as you will get to find a perfect investment environment. (Carson, 2014)

There several research organizations and websites to get the job market and local economy information. The following are some resources to obtain more insight into an area that may be good to invest in.

Business of Local Newspaper - this resource is invaluable to obtain information. The Business is full of reports and information about what's trending in the area that affects the community each day. Whether there's a new law office opening its doors, a shopping mall expanding and offering more stores to shop in, or a new hospital wing being opened, the local newspaper is the way to get daily news about the community.

Chamber of Commerce – this is an organization that invites local businesses in the area to join, meet and network with reputable businesses in the area. The Chamber is an ideal way of getting to know exactly what's going on, how business owners are affected by any changes happening in the community, and usually know the local economy, employment information and what they do to contribute to the community. The growth of businesses is encouraged, and the Chamber is supportive of its members. (Carson, 2014)

Local Realtor – this is really the way to getting the best information on what is going on in the real estate market in an area you are researching to invest in. Local realtors who work the area that you have wanted to find investments will be more than happy to share what they know about the market. They have knowledge about population growth, new businesses in the area, any rezoning that could affect the area and more.

Real estate professions watch the area trends, follow the housing market, sales pricing, and homes that have sold that may be in the price range and condition you are looking for. They know if there are any properties that are investments and whether they would be profitable as rentals or "rent-to-own" properties..

Realtors can obtain reports that are up-to-date because they are getting their information from their realty group's MLS. These reports give an overview of the neighborhood, school information, population, and other important community information. Reports also give the pricing of properties that are adjacent to a prospective investment property, as well as all other properties for sale in the area. Reports can be done by zip code, or by the circumference of an area. There is a multitude of ways that a realtor can key in on a specific neighborhood.

You have quite a bit to gain in forming a relationship with a realtor. If you feel this could be a good fit for both of you, continue to link up with them for future property investments.

Community Websites – city and county government websites that give a community or county overview can also be a fountain of information. They can supply population breakouts, any development plans and home sales in the area. You can use search engines like Google or Bing to search for specific community websites.

There is also a Comprehensive Plan that you can get by going to Google, Bing or any major search engine and type the location, i.e., Charlotte, NC, and the words "comprehensive plan" after it, and you will get planning for the next ten years and others up to the year 2040. You can also get the same information by typing in the county or county information will show up in the same search as a city search.

You will get information on planning, building, and development, building code enforcement, planning and zoning, and even stormwater and floodplain information. The last information is essential when you invest. You want to know the likelihood of a property possible being in a flood zone. If it is, then this would not be a property to purchase.

Real Estate Investors Group

Joining a real estate investors group can help to make the investment process easier. You'll be meeting and connecting with investors of all experiences – residential and commercial. These type of groups are always looking out for new investors and sharing information as well as their expertise.

Growth and Decline of Population

A stable community that is growing is one that investors look for when doing their due diligence and researching investment properties.

Employment and businesses impact the economy and are a link as to how people move from one area to another within their city, state or to another part of the country.

People move to where there are job opportunities. Not an easy feat, especially if they've been established in a community for quite some time and have to uproot their family and household to another place.

Other reasons for people motivated to relocate are rental and housing prices, interests, and activities such as skiing, boating or hiking, and the weather. The growth of population increases the demand for housing. When there is a high need for housing but a reduced amount, property value and rents increase. Following this kind of trend is where property investing can be lucrative.

Seeking Investment Areas

Actually, anywhere in the United States is good for real estate investments that can be profitable. However, as a beginner in real estate investing, starting in the neighborhood or the surrounding community is a good place to start. If you are thinking about investing out of state, it would be a good idea to wait until you have a few investments done before you take on a trickier long-distance transaction.

Your Neighborhood and Surrounding Community

You are now ready to begin to search for a property. You finances are organized and in order, did your research and made a decision on how you will be funding the investment, are pre-qualified for the funding, researched the communities you've thought to place you want to make an investment and attended a few Chamber of Commerce meetings and met a realtor you felt had the type of knowledge and experience you want to help you in finding the right property.

Earlier, the advice was given to start small when you invest for the first time. That covers a few points. Don't get in over your head, like seeing more than one property that you like and decide to buy both. Or you see a property on eBay that is an out-of-state property and make an investment. Multiple or out-of-state investments take time. As you gain experience and the capital to do so, you will be able to handle those types of investments. For the time being, searching for properties in your own neighborhood or in an area where the distance to travel is reasonable is the best way to start your search.

So, let's take a look at the neighborhood and community you live in. Does it fit the type of neighborhood you feel would be a profitable real estate investment? Are there possible properties that may need a little TLC in order to turn them into rental properties, or to "flip" them and sell them to a home buyer who wants to purchase the property as their primary residence? What about employment, job and population growth, affordability? If you get the majority of the list ticked off and it fits the parameters that have been set, then this is the best place for you to start.

Walk around your neighborhood or the community that you feel is the right one, to begin with. If you want to cover a wide area, drive around the residential streets, slowly. Take in the condition of the homes that are in the area. Are they well kept, lawns trimmed, trash free? Are there schools in the area? How far is shopping from the residential area – 2 miles, 5 miles? Are there supermarkets, restaurants, and major thoroughfares nearby?

Walking or slowly driving the area will give you a good feel of the physical conditions of the properties in the area. In doing this, you may find a gem that needs some rehabbing but has great possibilities for it to become a property the could be profitable.

If you find a property that needs work and the upkeep has not been done for a while, this could be a possibility for investment. It may be vacant, and, when checking with your realtor to ask if it's listed on the MLS, it may not be listed at all.

If you decide you want to get to know more about the property and approach it, knock first because there may be someone living in the property. If the owner comes to the door, speak with them and ask if they would consider selling the property. If so, don't automatically start talking price (unless the owner does and then, because you've done your research and homework, you will get a gauge about what kind of price they have in mind).

If they invite you to come in and see the property, make sure it's during the day so you will be able to see the condition of the interior. Ask questions about the property – how old is it, how long have they owned it, have they done any repairs, i.e., the roof, plumbing, etc. Look at the walls and the ceiling for water stains. If there are any, that means there have been leaks. Have they been fixed?

Be diligent in your inspecting, but not overtly obvious. Casually ask questions to get an idea about the property.

If the property is vacant, find out who owns it through a deed or tax records. If you still can't locate the owner, speak with the neighbors. There is usually someone who knows what happened to the owner and the property background. If you're persistent, making this find and turning it into a profitable real estate investment will make it all worth it.

Facebook – real estate can be found on Facebook.

People list their properties on a local buy site that is local and sell their properties. Usually, the properties are priced at market value, but there may be a few that you see that are not listed on the MLS because they are for sale by owner.

You may find a property that hits all the marks of being a possible good investment and beat out the competition.

Investing Preparedness

The preparations that need to be made before you invest in real estate can be a bit you overwhelming. However, once you've got it all in place, you can begin to invest and repeat the system you now have down over and over. When you go into real estate investing with organized finances, make the important decisions on how you will fund your first venture, are pre-qualified, have done your research of the community you feel is the right one to find your investment property, you will appreciate the experience and feel confident in creating a profitable real estate investment.

Property

Chapter 9. Finding Property

You are ready to find your first property!

Every investor remembers their first deal. It is often an experience you won't forget for a long time because it is the first time you will be acting. When you are set for this step, you will find a lot of options, and you may want to get in and buy the first property that catches your attention.

But hold on!

It is okay to feel excited about the idea of finally buying your first property, but you might be making a mistake when you buy the first property that pops in your radar. Before appending your signature on dotted lines, you've got to make sure you are making the right decision. Weigh other options and considerations as well.

Most first-time investors always wonder where they can search for properties. Well, there is a myriad of ways to do this, and each of the options will give you excellent prospects. Below you will find a comprehensive list detailing the places you can search for your first and subsequent properties.

Before you set out to look for a property, you've got to take the time to decide on an area first. Where do you want to invest? This step is very crucial as it helps you narrow down your search to a specific street, city or state.

If you are buying your first property, you are advised to settle for a property close to your home so you can easily keep an eye on the investment. Now, as you become more prominent and better at investing, you can spread your investments farther from you.

Make sure the area is one with great potential, if not now then in the future. Some areas are great for kids while some are perfect for the working-class individual who wants to live close to the city center. You don't want to buy a property you can't rent or sell, so the choice of an area is crucial.

If the area isn't good enough, you will struggle with the property long-term. If a property is located in an unsafe area, don't buy it. Think like your buyer or tenant when choosing a neighborhood. Don't be swayed by a good deal and the low amount to be paid for the property.

Now, onto the list of things to keep in mind when searching for a property:

The Value of the Property Should Come First!

If the location of the property isn't valuable, then you will have problems, so to avoid such issues settle for a house in a functional area. In addition to the choice of the city, look out for these key things when searching for a property:

- The neighborhood: What kind of people live close by the estate? Interact with some of them. If you can, spend time moving around to know what to expect of the place.

- Condition of the property: Don't allow the seller coax you into buying a property that is not in excellent condition. Set your standards high, and if a property doesn't meet the rules, move onto the next.

- The number of units: The number of units is essential, especially if you plan on renting the property to tenants. You've got to know if you will be getting high ROI from the apartments through rent.

- Appreciation potential: What is the possibility of the property selling well later? Will it increase in value with time? Is it valuable and will you have long-term gains from it?

With the knowledge of the area in mind and other factors you can start searching now.

Drive Around Your Preferred Location

Whenever you have the time, drive around the city. Take a drive and look around for the "for sale" signs. While driving around, take notes and pictures. When you get back home, look through the images and details you gathered before deciding on contacting the seller.

There are also a lot of vacant properties in some places, so keep that in mind. You can find out the landlords of such abandoned properties and reach out to them with an offer. There is so much you can discover while driving around searching for a house, enjoy the process!

Let Everyone Know You Are Searching

Aside from driving, you can also spread the word. This idea is like an old-fashioned way of searching for properties, but it works! Within your inner circle, community and the people around you, there will be others who want to sell.

Sometimes it may not be the person within your circle that wants to sell; it may be that someone around you knows someone else who wants to sell. But you will only be remembered when you put the word out.

When you are in a meeting or a gathering, talk about your investment desires with others. When one of the persons you tell have an opening of a listing, you will be the first to know.

Property Management Companies

Property management companies know all about listings and available properties in the best areas because of their contact with sellers. If you are looking for excellent investments, you might want to reach out to an agency.

Some sellers will not want to sell their properties directly by themselves, so they rely on such agencies. Now, when you have a relationship with a management agency, you will be getting briefs on properties for sale.

You will most likely get a seller to sell swiftly to you when dealing with a management company. Such companies know all about the state, cities, layouts, neighborhoods and streets. They can predict the future value of individual properties so you can make great investment choices.

Also, note that you don't always have to settle for only established and excellent properties. While dealing with a property management company, you should also inform them to send you briefs on properties on the market that require minor renovations. With such properties, you can buy them, invest in them through renovations and put the property back on the market at an increased price.

Email

With email, you get to send numerous messages to people who want to sell their properties. A lot of real estate investors see email as an older method, but it still works if you are consistent with it. Also, when working with email, you have to exercise patience because it will take a while to get that one good deal from the numerous emails you send.

If you send out 50 emails, you will probably get 20 replies with people offering their properties. You should narrow it down to the top 10 and then further down to the best 5.

How do you get the email addresses? Well, you can get a lot of emails from your website or the marketing efforts you implement.

So, you can succeed with email, but in addition to patience you will also need to enhance repetition and consistency. Don't expect good results when you send out emails for the first time, you will be introducing yourself to the recipients.

The second email will be a follow-up to the first one, and with this second one the recipients will become familiar with you and develop an interest in you as an investor. Then, you should be getting replies from the third email and subsequent ones.

Always take your time to the information you receive before making any significant commitment.

Craigslist

This platform is bulletin styled, meant for posting ads and buying/selling of items. The platform is not for real estate only, but you can discover properties because of agents posting listings for the audience.

You can go on Craigslist, look through and seek properties for sale in the market. You can also utilize Craigslist as a means to contact landlords directly.

Now, on Craigslist, when you encounter a landlord, you may not get a favorable response immediately. But the whole idea of using Craigslist is that it offers you a myriad of options.

Some landlords may insist that they don't want to buy, and they only want to rent.

When you encounter such landlords, don't worry. Build a relationship with them. Whenever they have another property for sale or when they have information for you, they will reach out.

So, think of Craigslist as a networking platform as well. Since many sellers post there, you will also be able to determine the top selling properties. You will even see the kind of houses most people prefer. Craigslist can be quite informative, so visit often and you will learn a lot.

Online Market

Everything is online these days, even properties. Sellers are online, and you can get fantastic deals on houses on the online market. The best place to start searching online is social media. There are lots of real estate influencers and pages dedicated to properties.

Someone else is trying to make sales on social media just like you will do when you are ready to sell. Use the right real estate hashtags to search for properties on sale, contact the sellers and complete the transaction from there.

If you have a specific area in mind, you can use the location feature on social media to search for what you need. While searching, save images and contacts so you can reach out when you make a final selection.

In times past, Facebook used to be the leading source for real estate ideas on social media, but today it is much more diversified. You can search on Instagram, Twitter, YouTube and other platforms with the assurance of getting great leads.

Isn't it amazing that we started with simple definitions, and now here we are with you ready to purchase your first property. We are going to go through the steps on how to make that property yours.

There is a buying process when you want to finance your investment and the below will provide insight into that process.

1.You reach out to the seller of the property indicating your interest to buy. At this initial stage, you are not negotiating; you are merely getting to know the seller and requesting an inspection and tour of the property.

2.Go to the property with an inspector who can verify the state of the property. Don't leave out any details at this stage because when you pay for the property, you will be responsible for any damage.

3.Screen the property through a list of criteria you set for your ideal property and other details you will need to ensure that the deal is secured.

4.This step is where you make an offer on the property. You can make an offer that is lower than what you wanted to spend initially. This offer is mostly made using a purchase and sales agreement, which a real estate agent can prepare for you.

If you are buying from the MLS, you won't need an agent. You can fill out the sales agreement online or you can get an attorney to fill out the sales agreement. Whatever deal you settle for, work closely with an attorney so you don't miss any details.

5.This step entails negotiations with the seller. At this point, you both will agree on a price and other terms.

6.Here, you are required to take on due diligence by inspecting the property. The details of the property are handed over to an escrow company or a

98

local attorney based on what applies to your state (the rules for real estate varies from state to state).

You will also need to submit all the required paperwork for your financing. This step may not be completed in a day, especially if the bank is responsible for your funding, as it often takes longer with the banks. But if you are using cash, then closing for the property can be faster than expected.

7.Next, you sign all relevant papers with the attorney present and the documents recorded several days later. Depending on your state laws, it might take a few days for the property to be legally yours. When you've completed all the paperwork, you will be the new owner of the property.

Now after, getting the legal part over with and obtaining the keys to the property, you must set your plans in motion and start deciding on what you want to do with it. Remember that the goal is to get your ROI.

We mentioned financing in step three, which is a significant core aspect of the investment process.

Chapter 10.   Low Cost Properties

What is the best alternative for your money investment? Generally safe investments that give an exceptional yield on investment, obviously! That is the reason such a significant number of effective investors go to real estate putting resources into rental properties.

Be that as it may, shouldn't something be said about the majority of the stories you've caught wind of real estate investors losing huge amounts of cash from rental properties? They're most likely racing into your brain as you hear "Purchasing rental property is perhaps the best choice for okay investments."

The reason these accounts exist. Each choice a real estate investor makes when purchasing rental property influences whether it will be an okay money investment or not. In this way, if a real estate investor does not adapt precisely how to discover generally safe investments when purchasing rental property, his/her real estate investment can come up short.

In any case, rental properties can be the best generally safe investments.

For what reason are rental properties the best Low Risk Investments?

Before figuring out how to discover okay investments when purchasing rental property, realize you're settling on the correct decision for your money investment. Investigate why rental properties are the best generally safe investments.

Investment Properties Generate Monthly Rental Income

When purchasing rental property is done well, a real estate investor can begin making positive income from rental salary inside the main month or something like that. No other generally safe investments enable the investor to begin making cash back on a money investment so rapidly without selling.

Investment Properties Are Tangible Income Producing Assets

The watchword here is "substantial". In the wake of purchasing rental property and checking the accomplishment through positive money flow (or scarcity in that department), a real estate investor can make a move and influence change. Having the option to control the accomplishment of a money investment makes rental properties generally safe investments.

Investment Properties Appreciate in Value

Other than profiting from rental pay, the estimation of investment properties will in general go up. Particularly in the present lodging market, which is a seasonally tight advertise all around, gratefulness will in general occur at a quicker rate. This implies selling these okay investments quite often ensures an exceptional yield on investment.

Steps to Finding Low Risk Investments When Buying Rental Property

We presently realize that rental properties can be generally safe investments, yet there are sure stages a real estate investor can take to guarantee he/she finds an okay real estate investment.

Step #1: Location in the Real Estate Market

The initial step is pinpointing the best places to put resources into real estate for generally safe investments. An area in the real estate market can influence everything about okay investments: their capacity to pull in inhabitants, cause rental salary, to create positive income, and sell for a decent rate of return. There are two to this progression when purchasing rental property: picking a city with a promising real estate market and finding the best neighborhood for investment properties.

The Ideal Real Estate Market for Low Risk Investments

A real estate showcase with the best places to put resources into real estate will above all else have a sound economy that displays work development. Search for a real estate advert that has new rising organizations or effective organizations that are growing or moving to the city. This will prompt populace development and an expanding interest for investment properties.

A real estate investor should investigate the unemployment rate of an area just as the enhancement of the business. An area subject to one industry could mean awful things for real estate contributing if that industry falls or migrates.

The real estate showcase you pick when purchasing rental property can really represent the deciding moment the arrival on investment. Search at an area with minimal effort to lease proportion for the best okay investments. A decent degree of profitability comes when a real estate investor can charge a decent lease value contrasted with the price tag of the investment property.

The Ideal Neighborhood for Low Risk Investments

Picking the best places to put resources into real estate doesn't stop at finding an incredible real estate advertise. The decision of neighborhood for investment properties is similarly as significant, as the real estate contributing potential can differ from neighborhood to neighborhood. In the event that you need a simple method for picking the best places to put resources into real estate, investigate the area to guarantee it advantageously has walkability and access to open transportation, low wrongdoing rates, and great school locale to guarantee investment properties will be generally safe in that area.

Step #2: The Condition of Investment Properties

When a real estate investor has discovered the absolute best places to put resources into real estate, it's an ideal opportunity to pick a genuine investment property. Perform investment property examination to choose which investment property will be a standout amongst other generally safe investments.

Investment property examination will help a real estate investor decide whether the state of the rental property will help in getting a decent rate of profitability or hurt its odds. The best generally safe investments in real estate don't require an excessive number of fixes, yet still, have some space for constrained appreciation. An investment property with restorative fixes like a requirement for new paint, covering, or another apparatus or two is a sheltered decision for your money investment.

A home ought to uncover what fixes are required. Investment properties with major auxiliary issues, rooftop harm or water and electrical framework harm won't make for okay investments.

Investment property investigation, just as home , ought to uncover the age of the investment property, which a real estate investor needs to contemplate when purchasing rental property. Why? The more established the investment property, the more upkeep and fixes it will require. Regardless of whether the home investigation uncovers no requirement for fixes now, an old investment property will require them soon, later on. Here is the manner by which to think about the ages of an investment property and the fixes required:

• 5-10 years of age: practically no upkeep

• 10-20 years of age: more upkeep

• 20-30 years of age: will require substantially more fix: rooftop, water warmer, funneling, and so forth.

Make certain to check the home report; more seasoned rental properties that have had a profound redesign as of late can at present be generally safe investments.

Step #3: Return on Investment

A system that guarantees general safety of investments is real estate contributing for positive income. On the off chance that a real estate investment has positive income from the beginning, a real estate investor will profit when an inhabitant is set up to give rental pay.

Positive income is the point at which the yearly rental pay of an investment property surpasses the majority of the costs required to claim and look after it (fixes, charges contract, and so forth.). Proceeding with investment property examination, a real estate investor must complete computations to decide whether there will be sure income for an exceptional yield on investment.

The best rate of profitability metric to use for investment property investigation is money on money return:

Money on Cash Return = (Cash Flow/Cash Invested) x 100

With a positive income, the money on money return estimation will demonstrate a positive rate of profitability. Real estate specialists concur that any investment property which can give 8% or higher will expedite a decent return investment and positive income.

Step #4: Exit Strategy

The last advance in discovering generally safe investments in the real estate market is ensuring a leave technique is set up before purchasing rental property. There are two principle leave procedures in real estate contributing:

• Buy and hold (long-term or present moment)

• Selling the investment property

Either leave methodologies ought to apply to generally safe investments effectively: one as the leave procedure to utilize quickly and the different as a reinforcement leave system, on the off chance that things don't go as arranged.

Rental properties can be generally safe investments for profiting in real estate. A real estate investor simply needs to make the correct strides when purchasing a rental property. Concentrate on the area, the state of the investment property, and the arrival on investment, and plan for a leave technique.

Great Rental Property Choosing Tactics

What would be a good idea for me to search for in an investment property? This is a typical inquiry for real estate investors. Figuring out how to decide a decent rental property will mean the distinction between a gainful investment and a terrible investment.

There are various elements that go into deciding whether a rental property is a wise investment. This article will disclose when to purchase dependent on market cycles, where to purchase, what kind of investment property to purchase, and what a decent return on an investment property is.

At the point when to Buy Rental Property

Understanding business sector cycles will enable you to choose when to purchase. To do this, you should almost certainly perceive if the zone you're taking a look at is an economically tight advertise or a wide-open market.

As we are hoping to purchase an extraordinary rental property, we need to purchase during a fast-moving business sector. A fast-moving business sector is when there are numerous homes available and not a ton of purchaser's – giving purchaser's everything the power. Purchase during a fast-moving business sector. Sell during an economically tight showcase.

Where to Buy Rental Property

Much the same as the climate, real estate is very area subordinate. The real estate market can be hot in one town and cold in the following. Indeed, even inside a similar city, you can have more than one real estate showcase. The area of a property is commonly viewed as the absolute most significant factor in deciding its worth.

You need to search for a property in a decent neighborhood, in a decent school area, near employments and nearby pleasantries. These components will probably build the estimation of your rental after some time – as long as these variables remain the equivalent.

The most effective method to Spot Good Locations

There are incredible markets everywhere throughout the nation. In each state, you can discover pockets of business sectors on the precarious edge of development. Here is a portion of the criteria we search for:

• Is it situated close to a major city? Enormous urban communities can extend employment opportunity expansion, alongside culture, nightlife and helpful comforts.

• How enormous is the populace and is it developing? Hope to put resources into urban communities with more than 1 million occupants. In many zones, around 40% of the populace rents, which leaves 400,000 potential occupants for your rental property.

• You don't need to purchase a property in a major city. The key is to take a look at a whole metro zone to decide the best neighborhoods. You may find that there is really a more noteworthy interest to purchase in the suburbs of a major city, where the rates are lower, schools are better and the enhancements are more pleasant. Try not to purchase excessively far away from the city as individuals for the most part would prefer not to live over 30 minutes away.

• Is it decent to advertise? Investors can decide whether the territory is encountering a purchaser's or economically tight showcase by checking stock levels and to what extent it takes for a property to sell (normal number of days on market, or DOM).

• Are home costs expanding or diminishing every month? A decent general guideline is to see home estimation drifts over a continuous multi month time span.

• Is there rental interest? Sites and neighborhood property supervisors can give data about rental interest in the region.

• Does the zone have a low middle or normal home cost? Middle home costs are essentially the widely appealing properties. In a moderate market,

109

the normal home cost ought to be close to 3 to multiple times the normal pay.

What Type of Rental Property Should I Buy?

There are various approaches to profit in real estate. You may put resources into a business property, mechanical property, a whole high rise or a solitary family home.

Whatever you choose is the best course for you, pick one, gain proficiency with the intricate details, stick to it and become a specialist. You can't do everything, in the event that you need to do it well. Pick the system that works for you and put your vitality into that by itself.

The single-family home is the least difficult approach to begin as another real estate investor. Furthermore, numerous master investors will reveal to you it's the absolute best investment in real estate. From our experience, the best kind of single-family homes have in any event 3 rooms and 2 showers.

When you consider what you search for in a home for your family, odds are it's a solitary family home and not a duplex, triplex, townhouse or condo. Single-family homes are much simpler to both lease and sell than multi-family homes.

In the event that you are attempting to sell a multi-unit property, no doubt different investors will hope to get it. As we understand, investors are continually searching for an arrangement and would prefer not to pay the maximum. While single-family homes can be offered to people in general at retail cost. If your property is reasonable to the normal purchaser, you ought to hope to have a lot of interest when you sell or lease.

This is particularly obvious when you've set aside the effort to purchase a decent rental property. Where it's situated in a decent neighborhood, with great schools, near occupations and access to nearby luxuries.

More reasons we like to put resources into single-family homes:

• Easier to upkeep

• Higher quality tenants

• Faster appreciation

• Easier Financing

• Affordable value focuses

Instructions to Analyze Investment Properties

When you're out taking a look at potential investment properties, it's essential to realize how to break them down. Accepting you've pursued our tips on where to get, you at that point need to run the numbers. This incorporates the anticipated lease and every one of the expenses or costs related. Remember to incorporate closing costs, escrow expenses, potential opportunity and home loan expenses.

While there might be a great deal of costs, make sure to consider month to month lease, energy about the property, yearly increment in lease and tax cuts you fit the bill for. Each and every time you take a look at a home, make a point to utilize your income investigation condition and let the numbers represent themselves.

After you've separated every one of the numbers, you would then be able to choose if this rental is going to accommodate your investment procedure and produce positive income. In case you're uncertain how to income returns on a property, visit our site to download a free income investigation spreadsheet.

To recap, here's the manner by which to decide a decent rental property:

• Located in an alluring territory close to occupations

• Ideally in a metro zone with more than 1 million individuals

• Single-family homes

• Well-kept up and refreshed

• Priced in the middle range for the zone

• Priced between $100,000 to $200,000

What is a Good Return on Investment Property?

Contingent upon who you ask, anything over a 15% ROI could be viewed as a decent return on a real estate investment. Be that as it may, there are a couple of approaches to precisely ascertain your potential rate of return.

Ascertaining ROI

The return on investment (ROI) is a measure used to assess the proficiency or benefit of an investment. As it were, the measure of return with respect to the investment's expense.

Return on initial capital investment = Annual rental salary/Total money investment

Computing Capitalization Rate

The capitalization rate or top rate is the pace of profit for a salary property dependent on the net operating income (NOI). The top rate demonstrates the pace of return considering your strategy for financing. Investors for the most part consider a decent top rate above 8%, and particularly 10%.

Top rate = NOI/Price

Computing Cash on Cash Return

A money on money return or COC return, measures the yearly return on your investment dependent on the NOI and the all-out money investment. Your COC changes relying upon various financing techniques. Generally, a great COC return is above 8%, yet go for above 10% or 12%.

COC Return = NOI/Total money investment

In contrast to the financial exchange, real estate is simpler to foresee, on the if you realize what to search for. To remain over market cycles in the zone your rental is found, you have to focus on any changes.

Essentially go on the web and search for school evaluations, nearby bosses, wrongdoing rates, rental rates, home rates and populace shifts. In the event that you notice negative things occurring around there, you can generally choose to offer your rental property before qualities start to diminish and purchase in a best in class neighborhood.

Chapter 11.   Negotiations

Now that you've made your offer and it's been accepted, the next step is negotiations. As this is not something you do every day and you may not be very comfortable in this position, but learning to negotiate is an art form and one that you will need to tailor as you travel down the investment path. You don't want to be the person who always pays full price or lays down for a high-baller. You want to be the top dog who always maximizes your cash flow. Let's get to work.

Negotiation Process

The next part of the process is a little harder and something you have no control over. Waiting for the seller to respond.

Picture this, you find a property you really like and want to make an offer on but as you research the comparables in the area you realize that the seller has overpriced the property. Let's say the building is priced at $550,000 but comparables in the area over the last six months have sold for between

$475,000 and $500,000 and upon some initial inspection you see that the property does need some work.

What now? Well, you could walk away. But you now like to see problems as challenges so instead you write up an offer closer to the low end comparable ($480,000) knowing you will have to do some repairs to get in ready for rental. The seller may ignore the offer or they may counter. For the sake of this example let's say they counter back with an offer of $540,000. Still higher than you would like but now you know the seller is willing to bargain.

Now you have a couple of options. Counter a slightly higher price than your original offer but still lower than they want and put in some data to prove why you are offering low, fixing the roof costs "x", the windows need replacing and the cost "x" so you're deducting that from the offer price. Or you can counter closer to what they are asking if they are willing to fix these issues before closing.

Again, for the sake of this example you counter with the first option, only slightly higher ($495,000) with the data to show the repairs that are required. The seller disagrees with your assessment and counters with $525,000 but willing to fix up a couple of minor issues.

We are getting closer.

You accept the minor fixes but still want the roof fixed before closing so counter one more time offering $510,000 if the seller will fix the roof and the other issues before closing.

The seller agrees. You are now the proud owner of a new piece of property.

So the seller will respond one of three ways:

- Accept it - Yay! This is the answer you wanted.

- Reject it - Boo! That's ok, now you can move on to other deals or wait and resubmit down the road.

- Counter it - Usually, the seller will come back an offer that is lower than their asking price but higher than your offer.

Coming back with a counter is a good thing. It signifies that the seller wants to sell to you, so it's best to see the positive side and try to meet in the middle so that both of you end up happy with the outcome. Never get too aggressive or insulting with what the seller counters with.

Think of countering as a way that both parties can walk away from the deal happy and having achieved what they wanted. These negotiations don't just refer to price. It also refers to the closing date, possession date, contingencies, closing costs, repairs, and many other things. Anything and everything can be on the table for discussion, the possibilities are endless.

When to Negotiate

The most intense and heated negotiations can happen immediately after submitting your first offer. You may take turns countering until one of you walks away or you start to meet in the middle and come to an offer that works for you both.

If the inspection reveals any kind of defects, especially one you weren't expecting, this is when you can back out if you have an inspection contingency in your offer or you can look at negotiating on the repair costs. Maybe you ask the seller to have the repairs fixed before closing, maybe you ask the seller to lower the price to make up for the repair costs you will have to spend upon closing.

The reality is negotiating can happen at any point along the process. Think about it this way, you negotiate every day in some small way, whether it is with your spouse, your kids or colleagues, negotiating a fair price is no different. It doesn't have to be at the beginning and it doesn't have to be after the inspection, it can be ongoing which builds more trust between you and the seller making them more likely to meet you halfway.

Tips for Successful Negotiations

• Always get the last concession, similar to getting the last word in a disagreement. For everything the seller asks for during the negotiation, you agree. Even if they want you to pay an exorbitant amount more than you offered, say ok but still only pay the closing costs. Always find a way to ask for something of the seller when they counter. Eventually, they will see that anytime they require something, so will you, this makes short work of dissolving any confusion.

• Knowing your role is important when in multiple-offer competitions. You don't want to come in guns blazing with your offer or concessions when the seller has three other offers on the table. You'll end up looking foolish before you even begin. Long story short, know what you're walking into and act accordingly.

• Negotiate with information and have comparables at the ready. When possible hit the seller with data you gathered about similar properties in the neighborhood, especially when you can't seem to find common ground on a price. It's hard to argue with facts and it may bring the seller down back down to earth.

● Use the tactic of gathering information to find out the seller's true motivations for selling. Are they looking for a quick close? Do they need to move and don't want to deal with an out of state property? Is it due to a spousal death and they simply don't need a big house or want to be reminded of the memories anymore? Whatever their reasons, try to appease them while still getting what you want in the process.

● Institute a penalty. When the seller comes back to you with concessions institute a penalty but that I mean taking your time to respond to their counter or if they counter with an amount higher than you want, you say fine but and add in something that you will expect for that higher price, and each time they ask for something, you also ask for something in return. Eventually they will stop asking for things as they will begin to realize that asking for things means possibly having to give up something else and could hurt their bottom line.

● Ask for their lowest price, then go lower. If you are negotiating with a motivated seller try asking what their absolute lowest price is. Usually, this isn't really their lowest number, but if you were to say "If I could pay you all cash and close in the next couple of weeks how would that sound?" This gives you a better shot at a successful purchase. In just a few short moments you will have been able to talk then down from their "lowest" price and potentially save yourself thousands of dollars.

● Real estate is all about the numbers. A seller wants to get the best dollar for their investment property and you want to get the best deal. If you run the numbers on a property and have offered the best you can to make a profit, divulge this information to the seller. It's hard to argue against the cold hard numbers.

Don't get offended, and always be ready to walk away. When you don't need something as much as the other person, your position becomes stronger, especially when they realize you will walk away if you don't get the right deal. This is easier to say than it is to practice, especially for new investors, but you need to try and remain unattached. If you become desperate for the deal you are lost. Remember this is a game so stay focused, don't get your feelings hurt and always keep it light-hearted.

Due diligence

Chapter 12.   Doing Your Due Diligence

Due diligence is something you must not overlook when it comes to real estate. It has to do with the research a real estate investor carries out before buying a property. The goal of due diligence is to ensure that there are no problem areas in a property before purchase. Make sure that you do a comprehensive inspection of the property after an appraisal.

There is a lot more involved in due diligence, which is not something you can point out at just a glance. You need to consider an array of factors that have an impact on the amount you can earn from a property. In this chapter, we will be taking a look at some due diligence tips which will ensure you get the best out of your investment.

Tasks Involved in Due Diligence

Due diligence helps you make sure that the property you purchase aligns with your numbers. Below are a few things you need to do before you complete a property purchase.

Do Your Research

Before you sign any document, ensure you carefully go through it in detail. Do a physical evaluation of the property, and analyze the cost of insurance. Check out the area's market trends and values and budget for unforeseen expenses. You need to be as detailed as you can all through this process to ensure you can get the most profit from the property if you do decide to buy. Make an exhaustive list of all the benefits and drawbacks of the property you are planning to invest in, and don't forget to analyze every area, even the ones that seem insignificant.

If you requested financing, ensure you do an appraisal, as it underlines a property's value. If you request a mortgage, an appraisal will also be required by banks and other lenders to make sure that the property is worth the value placed on it. If the property fails to align with the value once the evaluation is done, you won't get approval for the loan. However, this can be reversed if the seller agrees to cut down on the property's price to what has been evaluated as the actual value.

To inspect the property, you will require the services of a property inspector, alongside a skilled appraiser. The appraiser will be of help when it has to do with the needed enhancements, the size of the property, where the property is located, and so on. The appraiser will also do a comparative analysis of other properties similar to what you want to purchase in the area. With an appraisal, you can make certain that you don't pay more than a property's market value.

Do a Title Search

Before you close on your purchase of a property, do research on the title history. This will aid you in ascertaining the actual property owner before you make a purchase. This is important, as it will ensure you don't have problems with ownership later down the line. If the past owner does some work on the property, and does not make complete payment to the contractors who worked on the property, the owner will have to pay the lien on the property entirely before selling. If you don't know about the lien before you buy a property, you will need to clear off the debt before the title of the property can be cleared.

After you have done a comprehensive check, you need to send in an application for an owner's title insurance to ensure you don't fall into issues that you may not have seen while doing research on the title. Some of the problems could span from undisclosed heirs, the omission of deeds, forgery, recording mistakes, among others. By getting an owner's title insurance, you can safeguard yourself from liens that may arise after closing the deal. Any lien that was not identified which arises, will be sorted out by the insurance company.

Follow the Homeowner's Association Requirements

Before you purchase a townhouse, apartment, single-family apartment, or condo in specific regions, do research on the guidelines and rules put in place by the homeowner's association. When you have uncovered these rules, ensure you go with all of the stated requirements. As a property homeowner, there are strict rules and regulations put in place by the homeowner's association which you need to observe. These rules are put in place and enforced to safeguard the appearance of the neighborhood you are in, alongside its values.

For example, there may be a restriction on parking a recreational vehicle on the driveway. If you fail to go with these rules, you may need to pay a fine. This is why it is of the utmost importance that you go with the laws and regulations put in place by the homeowner's association.

Doing a Property Inspection

Carrying out an inspection on a property you want to purchase is something you can't overlook. This would be your final hurdle to ensure that the property you are trying to purchase is in great shape.

As stated before, it is in your best interest to get the services of a licensed inspector instead of doing it on your own. But you need to understand that there are moments home inspectors may not be perfect and fail to point out specific issues. Inspectors point out the things you need to repair and change, and even though this is very important, this is not all the information you require to make a decision.

There are other areas you may want to take note of as well, which include:

- The amount of water you can find on the property, alongside its quality.

- Make certain that there is no mold in the property.

- Lack of radon, or its existence in the property. This is because radon has been proven to lead to cancer.

- Existence of lead paint for properties developed earlier than 1978. This information is crucial for individuals who have children not above six years of age.

Making Preparations for a Property Inspection

Before the property inspection, there is a collection of things you need to make available. An easy way to do this is to outline all of the aspects of the property that require inspection. Some of the things that should be included in this list should span from:

- Doors and windows

- Exterior paint

- Rain gutters and downspouts

- Power outlets, electrical panel, and light switches

- Porches and balconies

- Walkways and driveways

- Steps, stairs, and railings

- Garage

- Foundation

- Walls, floors, and ceilings

- Roof

- Water heaters, faucets, and plumbing fixtures

- Basement

- Appliances

- Attic space

- Heating, HVAC system, thermostats, and cooling

The inspection lasts for only a few hours, and it is best to make yourself available while this is ongoing. Doing this will provide you with adequate data on the property's shape. Outline all of the vital things, take a few pictures, and ask questions about things you are not satisfied with.

Things Home Inspection Might Not Cover

The comprehensiveness of an inspection may differ based on the inspector. However, most inspectors are mostly interested in the physical features of the home. There are other areas you may need to inspect by yourself, which are:

- Pests that wreck wood such as carpenter ants and termites

- Fireplace and chimney

- Lawn sprinklers

- Floors obscured by carpeting

- Trees and landscape

- Internet and cell service

- Drainage

- Sewer lines

- Equipment for swimming pool

- Rodents, rats, and mice

- Odors

There are numerous considerations when inspecting a property you want to channel your resources into. We will now be looking into the forms of inspections you need to carry out before you buy a property.

Things to Inspect on a Property

Before you purchase a property to invest in, it is vital that you do not overlook inspection. Most lenders will request that you do an inspection before they offer you a loan, and as stated above, a licensed contractor or home inspector can help out with this. This can consist of a comprehensive account on the water heater, kitchen appliances, roof, and so on. The inspector will also offer an outline of all the spotted issues and how serious they are.

After carrying out a detailed inspection, it is not abnormal to spot some critical repairs you need to carry out, which will cost you a little extra. There are instances where the repair estimate will be so excessive that the buyer will have to walk away from the deal and find a more profitable option. This makes it necessary to accommodate cancelations in the buyer agreement after an inspection is finished. Also, you need to secure your cash deposit in the event you walk away from the offer.

Inspection for Wood-destroying Organisms (WDO)

Before you are provided with financing, many lenders will ask for this inspection to be carried out. Through this inspection, you will learn if the property's structure has a presence of wood rot. Various factors lead to wood rot, and some of these include water damage or termites. There is an array of areas you need to inspect which include the garage, interior walls, exterior walls, and so on. If there is a severe case of wood rot on a property, it could hamper the structural integrity of the property. The inspector will let you know how severe the wood rot is, which will help you determine if it is worth the risk.

Radon Gas Inspection

This kind of inspection is not a popular one. However, in the US, this specific gas is prevalent in numerous homes. The Surgeon General and EPA have stated that being exposed to this gas for long periods has been proven to cause multiple deaths each year through lung cancer.

Lead-based Paint Inspection

This is a form of inspection which is required by law for all properties developed in 1978 and before that. If a seller is aware that there is lead-based paint on the exterior or interior of a home, they are bound by law to inform prospective buyers.

Furthermore, it is still required by the buyer to carry out inspections of their own to be on the safe side. Lead-based paint can cause a lot of harm to the health of individuals, and it will require cash to get rid of before the home becomes habitable for individuals. The instant the inspections are over, the following are some of the options available to you:

- Reject the deal

- Go ahead with the offer after you have accepted the way the property is

- Request a better offer

If everything is satisfactory for you, then you can go ahead and sign an agreement with the property's seller. However, if there are minor problems with the property, you can ask to renegotiate the offer before you walk away. For instance, if the issues are small, you can request that the seller fixes them, or takes out the estimated cost of repairing it from the selling price.

Ground Rent

What is "Ground Rent?"

Ground Rent is very popular in the Baltimore Area.
Basically, the homeowner is responsible for payment of a small sum of money each year to the owner of the ground rent. Owners of ground rents can be private individuals, companies or banks.

Does the ground rent owner actually own my ground?
No.
The ground rent owner only owns the right to collect the ground rent.
They may not come on the property. The owner of the house is responsible for maintaining the ground. (snow removal, lawn cutting etc.)

How much ground rent do I have to pay?
The annual amount is stated in the original ground rent lease. Usually, yearly amounts range anywhere from $15.00 to $240.00. Payments are usually paid twice a year on the dates specified in the ground rent lease for one half of the yearly amount.
Most of the time, your mortgage company would pay the ground rent from escrow, similarly to the method of payment of taxes.

Can I buy (redeem) my ground rent?

Yes, normally ground rents for 99 year leases renewable forever are redeemable. The owner of the house has an automatic right to insist on purchasing the ground.

NOTE: certain ground rents created before 1888 may not qualify for automatic redemption.

How much does it cost to redeem the ground rent?

The amount to redeem your ground rent is based on the original ground rent lease and the laws of the State of Maryland. If the original ground rent lease states a redemption price, then the price is as stated. Otherwise, the Annotated Code of Maryland fixes the price as a capitalization rate. The capitalization rates are based on the date of the original ground rent lease and are as follows:

July 1, 1982 - Present - 12%

April 6, 1888 - June 30, 1982 - 6%

April 8, 1884 - April 5, 1988 - 4%

Prior to April 9, 1884 - Negotiable and possibly non-redeemable.

To compute the redemption price, simply take the annual ground rent and divide by the capitalization rate.

For example: Suppose the annual ground rent is $120.00 and created by a lease dated February 15, 1956. Using the above capitalization rate, $120.00/.06 = $2,000.00

Can the ground rent owner raise the price?

No, both the annual rent and redemption price are fixed by the terms of the lease.

What happens if I do not pay the ground rent?

This would be bad.

The ground rent owner does, after notice and a lawsuit, have the right to sell your house through legal proceeding to enforce the collection of the ground rent.

How do I find my ground rent owner?

The easiest way is to check the SDAT registration.

Step 1) Start at the SDAT website. Select your County and click "Street Address". Then enter the number and street name. Be careful not to enter the street name suffix (Road, Street, Avenue, etc.) Click on the Search button.

Step 2) Locate your ground rent owner by looking for the link at the top right corner of your property page entitled "Ground Rent Registration"

The Final Step: Run Your Numbers

After you have obtained all the needed information, the final step will have to do with running your numbers. In addition to your due diligence, this can help you determine if you should go ahead with the offer or walk away.

If after doing your numbers you find out that you can make a profit off property, then you can go ahead with your purchase. But what should you do when your numbers do not add up? Let's find out below.

What Should You Do When the Numbers Are Not Right?

As an investor, you do not want this. But if the numbers are not right after you do your due diligence, the following are the options available to you:

Request a price reduction

This is the first option available to you. Reach out to the seller and inform him or her of the discrepancy noticed in your number and request for contributions from them. If you can prove that you have observed problems that may have an impact on your overall cost, he or she should be willing to offer you a price reduction. In the case of REP deals, the bank will request that you showcase inspection reports or bids from contractors before they can provide a discount.

Reject the deal

If you are unable to get a price reduction, the next step may be to revoke the deal. This may not be satisfactory to all the parties involved, but there is no point investing in a money drainer.

Chapter 13.   Tax Implications of Real Estate

Investment

Most transactions, investments, economic activities and business attracts tax from the government, real estate investments and sales are not left out from this as there are tax rules covering the sector and they must be strictly adhered to avoid breaking a law.

Sometimes people make certain investments and enter certain businesses without fully educating themselves on the tax implications and tax benefits of what they intend to do. The government takes taxation very seriously, and as such, individuals should also take taxation issues seriously;

1. To avoid breaking a law and

2. To take advantage of tax benefits and allowance peculiar to your field.

There are certain tax incentives available to real estate investors, but only a proper knowledge of how tax works in relation to your particular investment choice will enable you to take due advantage.

The tax implications of real estate investments vary and are quite distinct according to the niche or category of investment. Also, the amount taxable is dependent on several factors including the type of investment, the worth or value of the investment, the profit earned from the investment, the income of the investor among others.

A knowledgeable investor who understands taxation will know how and when to legitimately avoid tax or significantly reduce the taxable amount. This can be either by selling off a property at a particular time or making certain expenditures.

Returns earned from real estate's investments normally is taxable under the income tax, while appreciation is subject to capital gains tax.

Income tax

Every form of real estate investment that is capable of earning an income, is eligible to be charged income tax. For example, a rental property that earns an income through rent paid by tenants is annually taxable. The final taxable amount is however dependent on certain factors and not just on the amount of rent generated.

In the case of passive investment options like mutual funds or REITs, were profits are received as dividends, profits shared are also taxable on individual investors earned dividends.

Capital gain tax

Capital gain tax is chargeable on the returns or profits realized from the sale of a real estate asset or property. A simple calculation of the capital gain tax is the sale price of the property minus the purchase price and any cost accruable from improvement or repairs.

There are usually two calculations for capital gain tax, they are;

- Short -term capital gain
- Long-term capital gain.

Short -term capital gain

This refers to gains or profits made on assets that are owned by an investor for less than a year. Normally they are taxed on the level of your annual income at ordinary tax rate within the investor's normal income tax amount.

Long-term capital gain

Long-term capital gain taxes are chargeable on assets sold after one year of retaining ownership. This operates quite differently from the short-term capital gain in that profits are taxed at a lower rate than the latter.

Capital gain tax benefit

Chargeable tax on a capital gain asset can be reduced, deferred or excluded, this is, however, dependent on certain factors. Some of the reason for a capital gain tax benefit can be the type of investment made, the number of years which the owner has owned or lived in the property, and what the capital gain was used for after it was earned.

For example, utilizing a capital gain in an exchange of similar property can defer tax payment.

Deductible expenses

This refers to a claim of expenses made by a seller or investor so as to reduce the taxable amount. Deductible expenses are legitimate ways to reduce the tax amount required of an investor to pay.

It is important to note that deductible expenses, does not include repairs made, they, however, cover other expenses like legal fees, real estate agent commission and other fees paid in the acquisition of a service that aided in the sale of the property.

This is a brief overview of what you should expect as tax while making your real estate investment; we recommend that you should seek the advice and knowledge of a tax advisor around the vicinity where you intend to make your investment. Sometimes tax rules differ according to location, investment type and other factors.

Chapter 14.   Conclusion

You are now on your way to financial freedom and building your real estate empire. I hope you now have a greater understanding of what it means to be a successful landlord.

But, before I leave you to go and start acquiring all your properties, a few last pieces of advice, as much as this book has talked about the "would be nice" apartment buildings, you should also consider the "wouldn't touch with a ten-foot pole" houses. There is no such thing as a perfect property, but there is sure to be one out there for you if you know what you want.

If you are on the hunt for your first property, then I sincerely hope this book has given you the inspiration you need to go out and start pounding the pavement to find that great house or duplex that will start you on your journey to financial freedom.

If you are a seasoned property owner, I hope you gained a little bit of knowledge you didn't have before, and this book inspires you to keep climbing.

What People Say About Us

"Our experience with "Investing in the United States" has been and still is extraordinary. We knew the founders a long time ago and we knew very well how professional, capable and above all transparent and clear they were. They have always come to meet our every doubt or question and have (and are continuing to do so) followed us step by step in making this excellent investment. The American real estate market offers a lot of interesting situations and Michele and Roberto are extraordinary in making you take advantage of the various opportunities that only a place like America can give. We strongly recommend the diversification of your assets by entrusting you to Michele and Roberto and we do not deny that, if the euro were to strengthen further, we would already be interested in a second investment. Congratulations again for the professionalism and the idea!"

"HIGHLY RECOMMENDED!!! I could not begin this brief testimony differently. I was looking for some real estate investment on the internet and I came across the site http://investireneglistatiuniti.com/ I wrote them an email, but without the conviction that something interesting could come out. Michele, seeing that I was asking for an investment abroad, addressed me and had Roberto contact me. Living abroad and not being able to go and meet them in their office to understand that it was not one of the many "buffaloes" that can be found on the internet, I immediately did some research on the internet about their company and Roberto. I immediately understood that it was not a "hoax". Just type Roberto on the internet to understand the reliability and seriousness of the person (I invite you to do it). But the thing that put me at ease the most was Roberto's way of doing. At the first chat on skype, Roberto, despite the poor internet connection, immediately wanted to activate the video to give a face to the person with whom I would have treated my investment. In the following chat on skype, in which he explained to me with a lot of patience and in detail everything there was to explain, he shared his pc screen and showed me several documents related to the investments and the various reports related to the leases. In short, although I live abroad, I did not know Roberto, none of my friends had ever collaborated with him, I must say that his way of doing and the fact that he put me at ease, beyond the enormous knowledge of the real estate and financial market made him give me all my confidence. I have recently become a happy owner of an apartment in Philadelphia and now we are considering the next investments to make. In short, what can I say, do not waste time, contact him for a cognitive chat and you will see that in a very short time he will be able to put you at ease and take the best care of your investments. You will then see that buying a house in the U.S. is very simple and feasible in a few exchanges of mail, as well as set up a company and open a current account. If you want to contact me for a live testimonial please ask my skype contact. Good investment to all. "

"I have been on the road to U.S. real estate investment recently, but at the moment I can only consider myself satisfied. Simplicity of management also from Italy, ridiculous bureaucratic load for our parameters, high returns. The thing that struck me the most is the transparency: through a few clicks I was able to verify the existence of the property and the history of its transactions".

"I've always been skeptical of investments, every time it was a question of entrusting my money to someone who would be able to "make it pay off". Every time I trusted these "specialists" I lost money. I arrived at Roberto by chance, through Google and I immediately noticed a difference: Roberto answers questions, he doesn't pull back, he doesn't climb on the mirror. This gave me confidence and pushed me to move forward. For the first time, thanks to him, I made an investment whose logic and risks I understand. His support is punctual and rigorous, it is a pleasure to communicate with him".

"I was completely skeptical and I remained so until I saw with my own eyes the simplicity with which I was accompanied and supported by Roberto and Michele in facing this type of investment that today generates constant monthly flows without any worries. At the beginning I was very worried, also because you can imagine the understandable mistrust to face this kind of operation without going on site and without ever even being there!

Today, after some time, I am extremely satisfied with the investment that I recommend everyone to make!"

"When I became aware of this investment proposal my reaction was extremely hesitant because I immediately thought about the possible problems that I would have to manage. Who does the contract? If there are problems with the condominium do I have to go to the site every time? And if the tenant does not pay me how do I manage the situation? Even in hesitation, skepticism and fear I trusted and trusted the support of Roberto and Michele. Today, some time after the conclusion of the operations, I am extremely satisfied from every point of view and I am building an integration to what will be, if ever there will be, my future pension. Very probably as soon as I will have the possibility to evaluate another purchase!"

"I landed on Roberto and Michele's site after a negative experience in the real estate field in Italy where, due to a tenant who was not paying, I was able to return in possession of my property in Milan after almost two years of hard work with lawyers, law enforcement and many bellyaches. After experiencing helplessness in front of the Italian bureaucracy I decided not to face this kind of investment anymore. Luckily I am a curious person and during my research on the web I found the website https://investireneglistatiuniti.com/ of Roberto and Michele on which I started reading some information about real estate investments in the USA and I realized that, absurdly, what had "cheated me in Italy" could not cheat me in the USA.   From there I continued to read looking for more and more information also on other sites and I decided to go deeper into it. During the research on the web, however, I realized that having little time available I would have to rely on professionals to deal with it because alone it would have been really hard. Among my researches, Roberto and Michele's website was the one that most gave me the impression of being supported by serious people with the aim to really meet the customer's expectations so I decided to face the first telephone contact. The confirmations arrived since the first phone calls where I felt followed with professionalism by Roberto and all my doubts and perplexities were dispelled. The fact that Roberto and Michele already had several properties in the U.S.A. immediately made me understand that they were not the classic "sellers" who sell something they don't believe in but on the contrary they were professionals who, by investing their time and expertise, had found a way to make an investment in the U.S.A. easy even for a person like me without experience overseas. After investigating the various possibilities with Roberto we identified a property that was right for me and within a few days we moved from theory to practice and I bought it. I absolutely recommend the approach to this type of investment with Roberto and Michele because everything that was proposed to me on paper also happened in reality. The returns are really higher than in Italy, the risks are much lower and the certainty of having two really competent and helpful people to support me is a real icing on the cake. I would absolutely recommend them because I was really followed step by step and thanks to them I now own my first property in the USA. In particular I would like to thank Roberto who was able to answer with promptness and determination to all my doubts even at times that are certainly not office hours! Thanks again!"

"I decided on this type of investment to diversify my portfolio, considering it appropriate to invest a portion of my assets in real estate. I trusted to invest in the U.S. because of my previous knowledge from a professional point of view with Dr. Roberto D'Addario and because together with Michele Brizi was able to create a type of diversification in real estate in the U.S., automating everything without being present throughout the negotiation going to America. What was necessary was done online via skype with all the explanations of the case. Once the negotiation that lasts less than a month, the following month you already receive the rent without worrying about anything; this is because on the other hand there are figures like the Property Manager who manage everything. I recommend this type of investment because, among other things, it falls within the perspective of capital diversification with excellent returns on investment and also because you are always followed by experts in the field of great experience. Many thanks to Dr. Roberto D'Addario and Michele Brizi for this great opportunity and for the work done with great humility and dedication, very good indeed".

"I contacted Investing in the U.S. to invest in the U.S. real estate market attracted by the opportunities that the U.S. market offers today. The impression I got from talking to Roberto was very good because, analyzing my financial situation, it made me understand that compared to my asset situation the investment would not be appropriate and it was better to evaluate alternatives. In absolute freedom and free of charge, I therefore received support from Roberto adequate to my needs without anything being sold to me contrary to what happens in other situations. I appreciated this way of working, even though I did not buy anything, as I found a great personal, professional and above all moral seriousness".

"I met Michele and Roberto a few months ago, while I was looking for a real estate investment abroad and they immediately gave me confidence and great professionalism. So I wanted to deepen the discussion and they explained to me with maximum transparency the whole "bureaucratic" process to buy a property in the United States. I am an operator in the real estate sector and I am used to real estate investments, but when you buy a property overseas without even seeing some little unconscious resistance comes to the surface. So I decided to Rely completely on Roberto and Michele confident of their skills and their seriousness and today, a few months later, I find myself with my real estate investment in the United States that generates a constant income. I would like to say a word for Roberto who followed me directly during the economic transaction and who brilliantly solved a big problem caused by the banks. There are many people who offer their services when it comes to investments and they all seem to be great professionals, but it is in times of difficulty that you can see the true value of a person, both on a human and professional level and I can assure you that Roberto and Michele have demonstrated with the facts that they are number one".

"Proud to collaborate with this wonderful company made of wonderful and very special people! Ten and praise!"

"A special thanks to Michele Brizi, very helpful and professional.

Well prepared in real estate, I recommend it to everyone."

"We wanted to thank Michele Brizi and the whole FEM group for the willingness and professionalism they showed towards us, illustrating and preparing the way to buy our first house.

Compared to other professionals in the sector, they put you at ease and show you all the possibilities to get to the purchase thinking practically everything about them. Congratulations!"

"You are very good, thank you for all the TRANSPARENCY and availability. Today we have done the deed and I can already go to live thanks to your professionalism. We even did the turn of gas, electricity and water. Thank you for this happy story of my life."

"Availability and perfect work at 360 degrees!"

"Professionalism, transparency and assistance from competent people. From the search of the house to the purchase with the possibility of extraordinary and/or ordinary maintenance."

"Thanks again for the extreme professionalism and competence with which you have accompanied us from start to finish, with you a dream has come true!"

You can find these and other testimonials on the website:

www.investireneglistatiuniti.com

About the Author

Michele Brizi was born in 1979 in Italy in a small Tuscan village: Sansepolcro, the birthplace of Piero della Francesca, Luca Pacioli and near Caprese Michelangelo where Michelangelo was born.

Passionate about houses and real estate investments from an early age, thanks to the real estate properties of parents and relatives.

After the scientific high school and the degree in Economics at the historic and prestigious University of Bologna, achieved in 2002, he continuously and constantly trained with all the best Italian and American trainers.

Immediately after graduating, he has been working in the real estate sector since 2002, starting from working in the accounting and financial part, then to the sale, in particular of houses under construction, and finally to real estate investments.

In 2005 he studied with the N.A.R. (National Association Realtors) and is passionate about the American real estate market.

He has advised many Italian investors to buy income homes in the USA and has made many real estate transactions and investments in many cities of the USA such as Chicago, Columbus, Philadelphia, Baltimore, Tampa and Orlando in Florida.

Real estate auction and real estate marketing expert.

He sold many houses in one day thanks to the winning formula of the "Open House".

Married and father of two sons, he divides his time between work and family.

Together with two other professionals, he created a complete video course on buying income homes in the USA, you can ask for more information about this.

If you want to learn more, if you have real estate problems to solve or simply get in touch with him, he is available for real estate consultancy.

You can contact Michele Brizi on Skype: michele.brizi

By email: michele.fem@gmail.com

Or by SMS or WhatsApp at: +39.347.1193614

CPSIA information can be obtained
at www.ICGtesting.com
Printed in the USA
BVHW041022071220
595087BV00007B/292